A Quiet Desperation

A Quiet Desperation

by
James W. Bennett

THOMAS NELSON PUBLISHERS
Nashville • Camden • New York

Many names, locations, and circumstances have been changed to protect the identities of certain individuals described in this book.

Published in Nashville, Tennessee, by Thomas Nelson, Inc. and distributed in Canada by Lawson Falle, Ltd., Cambridge, Ontario.

Printed in the United States of America.

Scripture quotations noted KJV are from the King James Version of the Bible.

Scripture quotations noted RSV are from the Revised Standard Version of the Bible, copyrighted 1946, 1952, © 1971, 1973.

Library of Congress Cataloging in Publication Data

Bennett, James W., 1942–
  A quiet desperation.

  1. Bennett, James W., 1942–   . 2. Mentally ill—
United States—Biography. 3. Anxiety—Patients—United
States—Biography. 4. Christian life—1960–
—United States—Biography. I. Title.
RC464.B44A36 1983   616.85′223   83–11400
ISBN 0-8407-5847-2

Foreword

So many of the books I read recounting how faith solved someone's personal problems seem to me superficial, and tenuous in their grasp of what Christianity has to say about the maladies of the spirit. The pearl of great price is a spiritual biography that recognizes there are no quick fixes for a truly troubled soul, that healing doesn't arrive with tomorrow's mail. *A Quiet Desperation* is such a book.

James Bennett's awful and prolonged experience of "fear and trembling" came close to devastating his life. It was nameless, deep-rooted, and beyond the curative powers of psychological counseling, pious formulas, or positive thinking. How he endured, his desperate search for answers and healing is a fascinating story. Essentially, though, this is a story of Christian hope and Christian victory.

He tells us that one day it came to him that he was in the process of becoming a Christian. This, it seems to me, is authentic Christian experience. One of the words Saint Paul uses for "salvation" means an ongoing process that never ends in this life. *A Quiet Desperation* is a witness to this Christian truth. It will appeal to you, as it does to me, as authentic. This story has the ring of reality about it.

Charles Merrill Smith

Preface

*T*his is my story.

I am not a celebrity or a famous person, or even a person of reputation on a small scale. Yet I have an important story to tell. This is the story of my mental breakdown and how I survived it.

It is the story of how I learned to know myself and how I made a new beginning. It is the story of my growth in the faith, and my new life in Jesus Christ. It is not a story of despair, although I was often desperate. It is a story of survival and hope.

My story will have meaning for you if you have ever suffered—or if you love someone who does suffer. It will have meaning for you if you are anxious or depressed or afraid.

. . . if you ever do any counseling.

. . . if you want to be a better listener.

. . . if you want to strengthen your faith.

. . . if you want a deeper understanding of the people around you and why they do the things they do.

. . . if you want deeper relationships with those important to you.

. . . if you want to understand better the potential of Christian community.

There are no simple answers or simple problems in my story. It was a long and complicated process that eroded my mental health, and the road back is also long and complicated. It is a road that I am still on. Yet it is a road I believe is leading to deeper faith, a closer walk with Jesus Christ, and thus, personal wholeness.

Hard as it is for us to accept, life is a process. It is not overnight that we create our problems, and seldom are we healed of them that way. I am in partnership with Jesus Christ in the healing process. I do not expect the process to end tomorrow, or next month, or next year. Stories end; they have conclusions. But a process is an ongoing situation. You, too, are a person in process.

If this story helps you, then it is a success.

One

*I*n early January 1974, my wife, Judy, our little son, Jason, and I returned to our home in New York state. We had just finished spending the Christmas holidays with my wife's family in Rock Island, Illinois, and also with my own family in Springfield, Illinois. It was a very satisfying holiday visit, as our eleven-month-old son saw his grandparents for the first time and thoroughly enjoyed them.

Two days later, something snapped.

I woke up that morning, filled with fear. Even before I got out of bed, I was overcome with terror and panic. I sat up on the edge of the bed and planted my bare feet on the cold, wooden floor. I shook my head as if to clear it—something was terribly wrong! I had simply awakened as on any other day, but feelings of terror ripped at my stomach.

"What the hell?" I blurted out.

I got out of bed. My stomach was constricted. I felt my pulse; it was very rapid. My palms were wet and clammy, and my fingers were cold. I was short of breath, and my heart was palpitating.

I was terrified. I was in a panic.

But what was the cause? I thought about my life; there was nothing unusual happening. And there was nothing special happening that day. It was just another day, but the terror was *incredible*.

I shaved and brushed my teeth, but I had to pause twice to lean on the basin and catch my breath. My stomach was contracted with such force that I was having trouble breathing, and I felt nauseated.

Downstairs at the breakfast table, Jason was smearing his cereal around on his high chair, and Judy was mixing orange juice. I went to where she was standing at the counter.

"Something's wrong," I said.

"What? What's wrong?"

"I'm not sure . . . I just have these feelings."

"What feelings?"

"Well, I'm not sure how to describe them. Fear, I guess. I have these feelings of fear all knotted up in my stomach."

She looked puzzled. "What are you afraid of?"

"I'm not sure . . . I don't know. Is there something going on? Is there something happening that I've forgotten?"

She shook her head. "There's nothing going on that I know of."

My stomach contracted even more. "Then this is absurd!" I snapped. "You can't just be afraid with nothing to be afraid of!"

"Is there anything unusual happening at school?" she asked.

I shook my head. "Not a thing. Nothing. I thought about that, and there's nothing happening."

With no success, I tried to eat some breakfast. I forced down two mouthfuls of corn flakes and drank my orange juice. It was nearly impossible for me to swallow—it was as if I had a block in my throat. My mouth was dry, like cotton.

I got ready to leave for school, stomach still churning in

panic, and I was angry. "Something weird is going on here!" I protested.

"Don't let it get you down," said Judy. "You'll figure out what it is."

I kissed her and Jason good-bye. "Don't let it get you down," Judy repeated.

The day was cold and bleak, with a heavy gray sky that looked like metal and a sharp January wind. I drove the five miles to the college where I taught English. Our offices were on the third floor of the administration building, an old and elaborate stone mansion.

In the lounge, many of the teachers were drinking coffee, laughing, and swapping stories of how they had spent their Christmas holidays. I tried to drink coffee, but I was still knotted up with fear. I listened to some of the conversations, but without hearing.

The third-floor lounge was a large and elegant foyer that had once been a ballroom. I walked across the room and read the notices on the department bulletin board. One of the notices read, "A Memorial Service for Mr. Hoak will be held in the student union auditorium at one o'clock this afternoon. Classes will be suspended during that hour. Everyone welcome."

I reread the notice in disbelief. Ed Hoak? A memorial service? I turned to Arthur, a very dear friend. "Arthur, what's this about Ed Hoak?"

"Oh, you haven't heard. He died over the holidays. It was a heart attack; it happened very suddenly."

The news stunned me. It shook me badly. I had been friendly with Ed, but never close to him. Now a new terror passed through me like an electric jolt. I went into my office, which opened off the lounge, and closed the door. I sat alone for some time, my heart fluttering.

I had three classes that day, and I functioned fairly well

in them. The level of fear that was contracting my stomach may have lowered, for I had well-prepared lecture notes and thus was able to get caught up somewhat in the classroom setting. The students were alert, and I had no difficulty answering their questions.

After class, however, when students stopped me for informal questions, I felt new fear grabbing at me, and I couldn't concentrate. I dismissed the questions as quickly as I could and went back to my office. I had to urinate frequently.

At lunch, I sat with my colleagues in the cafeteria. I was still gripped with such fear that I couldn't eat. I bought a macaroni salad and a Pepsi. I forced down a few of the cold macaroni noodles and drank half of the Pepsi. My friends swapped more holiday stories and talked of Watergate, which was just emerging as a national crisis. I did not participate; I couldn't concentrate and I couldn't sit still. It was very clear to me that something was desperately wrong.

After lunch, I went to the memorial service for Ed Hoak. The auditorium was an old theater with a full stage in front. Approximately one hundred students were there and about half as many faculty. The theater's capacity was three hundred.

I took a seat in a corner near the front. The lighting was dim throughout the auditorium, and particularly so where I chose to sit. I did not want to sit in the light or near anyone else.

First there was a hymn, "O God Our Help in Ages Past." Mrs. Robinson played the piano. I tried to sing, but my throat was constricted and tears sprang to my eyes.

A wooden lectern stood at the front of the stage. The first person to speak was Ken, a history teacher who was also a Unitarian minister. He spoke quietly of Ed's cheerful disposition, his positive attitude, and his beneficial effect on teacher and student morale.

The next speaker was Father Dale, a Roman Catholic priest who was also a science teacher on our faculty. Father Dale spoke with a sincerity that moved me. "Ed Hoak was too young to die," he began. "He was only forty. He was a vital and active person. The death of such a person is very hard for us to accept."

Father Dale paused and looked around. He was young and capable, and he spoke earnestly and openly. I envied him because he seemed so competent, while I was so shaky. He went on: "There is nothing we can do here to help Ed Hoak, for he doesn't need our help. My faith tells me he is now in the hands of the Lord, and we can't improve on that. But perhaps his family needs help, and help that we can give."

I looked across the way at Ed's wife and two teen-age sons. They were white and still. I felt a great sadness.

Father Dale went on to remind us that our support would be very important to Ed's family, and that we would have many opportunities to give such support. Then he led us in the Lord's Prayer. After that was a final hymn, "How Great Thou Art," and then the benediction.

I sat still in my seat as everyone else filed out. I wanted to be alone. A terrible sadness mixed with the fear in my stomach. Finally, everyone was gone and the lights were put out. I was alone in the dark auditorium.

I began to cry. I sobbed and sobbed, and the tears ran down my face and into my lap. I tasted the salty tears in my mouth. I felt wretched, and I didn't know why. Something very frightening and mystifying was happening to me, and I couldn't understand it. Oddly, I looked at the sleeves of my trench coat and saw that they were too short. This fact struck me as very pitiful, and I cried even harder.

After twenty minutes or so, I pulled myself together more or less. I went downstairs to the lower level of the union, to the men's restroom. I wetted a paper towel and washed my face over and over. Then I went into one of the toilet stalls, closed the door, and washed my face twice more.

At three o'clock I had my last class of the day. A fine snow was blowing in the air as I walked across campus to the classroom building where most of the humanities classes met.

I just barely got through that final class. Even as I was lecturing, the panic tore away at my insides, and on several occasions I almost gathered up my books and notes and left the room. Once I felt dizzy; I sat on the table at the front of the room to keep from falling. Somehow, I saw that class through to its conclusion.

I drove home in terror. When I got there, I spilled it all to Judy.

"What are your feelings like?" she asked.

"I'm terrified," I blurted out. "I'm terrified, and I don't know what about."

"Was there anything unusual at school today?"

I told her about the memorial service for Ed Hoak, and tears formed in my eyes as I told her.

"Ed Hoak wasn't a close friend of yours, was he?"

"No, not at all. I knew him, but we were acquaintances more than friends."

Judy was puzzled, and she frowned. "Let's have some coffee."

She made the coffee, and I started a fire in the fireplace. We sat at the dining room table drinking coffee.

"This can't be happening," I said quietly. "It can't be happening. I just can't be terrified of nothing."

For a while, Judy was silent. Then she asked, "Is there anything going on in your life that I don't know about?"

I looked at her. "What do you mean?"

"Is there anything you haven't told me about? Anything that might be causing these feelings?"

"I've told you everything," I said impatiently. "I'm not

having an affair. I haven't got a drinking habit. I haven't been gambling with our money. If there was something, I would have told you."

"I'm not accusing you of anything, I'm just trying to help."

"I know."

"I don't think you are hiding anything, but maybe there's something happening that you never thought important enough to tell me about. Maybe if there is, it could be more important than it seems."

She was trying to help, but the longer these fears worked on me, the more anger I felt. "I'm telling you there's nothing. I've thought of everything I can think of. If I thought of something, I would tell you."

"Jim, there has to be something."

"Of course there has to be something! You can't be terrified of nothing!"

She was hurt by my anger. My loud voice woke Jason from his nap. He was calling for Judy from his bedroom upstairs. "I'd better go get Jason," she said.

Still angry, I stomped out the front door and slammed it behind me. Without a coat, I stood in the cold and snow for as long as I could stand it. Then I went back inside.

At supper, I still could not eat. I spooned down a couple of bites of red gelatin and drank half a bottle of Pepsi.

I went to bed at the regular time, right after the late news, but I spent the night without sleep. Hour after hour I tossed and turned in terror. The night seemed to last forever. Just after dawn, I dozed for a few moments.

That morning was the same as the previous one. My stomach knotted up in terror. My heart pounded. I was short of breath and my hands were sweating. I was exhausted; my eyes burned from lack of sleep, and my head ached.

I went through another dismal and mystifying day.

I drove home after school and went straight to Judy. "I've got to get to the bottom of this," I announced.

"I'll do my best to help you," she said.

"I don't know where to begin," I said.

"Let's take each part of our lives, one at a time. O.K.?"

I sat, shaking with panic, and we searched for a cause.

"Could it have anything to do with your job?" she asked.

"I don't see how," I replied. "My job is secure; I've got tenure, and nobody that I know of is dissatisfied with my work."

"Is there any promotion you want or think you ought to have?"

"No, nothing."

"Is there anyone in the department you're having any trouble with?"

"No, not a soul."

"Are you having a conflict with a student?"

"Nothing more than the usual stuff about late papers and makeup work."

"Well, then, let's try money."

"You know our finances," I said quickly.

"Is there anything we want badly that we can't afford?"

This was a new idea to me, so I thought about it for a moment. "I can't think of anything. How about you?"

She shook her head. "No, I can't." Judy is a systematic person and, unlike me, very good at taking "one thing at a time." What was happening to me was obviously scary and disorienting for her. She was trying very hard to take a calm and analytical approach.

She went on: "Do we owe anybody any money?"

"You know we don't," I said.

"Is there any large expense coming up that we have to face up to?"

"No."

She thought for a moment, went into the kitchen, and fixed a cup of coffee for each of us. She sat down again with me, at the dining room table. "Is there anything in our family that could be causing these feelings?" she asked.

I looked at her. "Not as far as I know. We love each other, and we love our son. In my opinion, we are a happy family."

"I think you're right," she smiled. "How about health?"

"Yours is good, mine is good, and Jason's is good. We have no health problems."

I pushed my coffee away. We went across the room and sat on the couch, next to the corner fireplace. I put my arm around her, and she held me. I was terrified. We sat together for some minutes, and then she said, "What about your friends at the college? Do you feel separated from any of them?"

I shook my head sadly. I had gone over all of this in my own mind. "No, I'm not having any problem with any of my friends. None at all."

Judy shook her head, puzzled.

After some time, we went back and finished the coffee, at the table. I looked at my two hands gripping my coffee cup. Nothing. Absolutely nothing.

Then why was my stomach contracted with a nameless dread? What was making me sweat and shake? What was causing the perspiration drops to pop out on my forehead?

The terror continued for the next several days and nights. It was mysterious and sickening. Literally. Each night I went sleepless, trembling in bed. My pajamas were soaked with sweat. Judy would lie beside me, sleeping soundly while I curled into the fetal position and shook with fear, hour after hour until dawn, when I would try to face another day. It did not seem possible that my life could have taken this turn.

There is something especially frightful about suffering alone through a night of no sleep, and also something humiliating. As I lay there shivering, I often thought of an essay I had read on the value of a liberal education. I couldn't remember the author's name, but I remembered he had divided a person's day into three eight-hour parts. There were eight hours of sleeping, eight hours of working, and eight hours of leisure time. The point of the essay was that a well-developed mind would know how to fill the eight hours of leisure with creative activity.

The essay had casually dismissed the eight hours of sleep by pointing out that "Any human being, intelligent or otherwise, should have no problem with that eight-hour period."

Well, *I* was having trouble with those eight hours. I was spending them awake and afraid.

In the middle of the night, I would begin to imagine all kinds of fearful things. Was I losing my mind? Was I breaking down completely? Would I never recover?

I was going to die; that was it. My terror would continue until my body just couldn't take any more. Then I would just die, probably of a heart attack. It could happen while I was sitting at my desk, or while I was driving the car. It could happen anywhere, or any time. I pictured myself dead at my desk, my friends finding my body slumped over it. I pictured myself dead in my car along the side of the road, my body slumped on the steering wheel.

I feared that I was coming unglued. I was going to become feeble-minded. I would be locked up in a state mental hospital. I saw myself in a padded room in an asylum—a room with bars on the windows. I shivered in bed as I saw myself, several years hence, locked up in a mental hospital. My wife and son would come to visit me, their eyes full of shame and resignation.

My mind manufactured one fearful proposition after another: I saw my son at the age of sixteen, loathing and rejecting me. I pictured my wife walking out on me in disgust, taking our son with her.

The sleepless nights were long and lonely. My mind was out of my control. It seemed to run as if on its own power source.

Some nights I would feel a sense of shame and go to the guest bedroom. There I folded down a small metal cot, which was very narrow. I lay in it alone. Some nights I cried and cried.

One night, in panic, I went downstairs. I had to move around. Our house was two hundred years old, with the original wooden plank floors. There was no carpeting, and the floorboards were cold on my bare feet. I sat on the couch and stared out the window at the neighboring farmhouse, some one hundred yards to the northwest. The pole light was burning in the farmyard; otherwise the night was very dark. It was snowing and blowing, a fine, powdery snow flying across the snow crust that covered the ground. The wind whistled at the windows. My eyes burned. The landscape seemed dark and lonely and desolate. I felt terribly alone.

Some nights, just when it seemed as if I might be about to drift off to sleep, the neighbor's farm dogs would begin to bark and I would be awake for the rest of the night. I was gripped in a desperate cycle: I couldn't sleep because of the terror I was feeling, and my lack of sleep made the terror worse. I was exhausted, but unable to sit, stand still, or relax. It was as if my body had been wired with an electric current.

One afternoon, following another sleepless night, I went to a drugstore. I wanted to buy some sleeping pills and some ear plugs. I thought if I could just get some sleep, I could attempt to deal with those feelings.

I made certain to go to a drugstore where I had never

been before. In the store, I pretended to be looking around at merchandise. I was ashamed to be buying sleeping pills and ear plugs. I was ashamed because I felt that only a neurotic would need sleeping pills.

I saw several types of sleeping pills on the counter. They all cost about the same. I chose a bottle of Sominex and a bottle of Sleep-Aid; I don't know why I took one of each. Then, as if to disguise what I was doing, I picked up several other items that had nothing to do with sleeping. I picked up some gum, a candy bar, and a lip balm. I also got *Time* magazine. There were no ear plugs anywhere that I could see.

I took all my items to the pharmacist behind the counter. He began to ring up the items. I made myself ask for the ear plugs: "I was wondering if you have any ear plugs?"

"Ear plugs?" he asked. He was a pleasant young man with dark-framed glasses. "Yes, we have ear plugs. You want them for sleeping or for swimming?"

Ashamed, I said, "For sleeping."

He reached under the counter and pulled up a small, orange box. It said "Stopples" on the cover. Then he rang up the rest of the order. Before I left the store, I made sure all the items were concealed in a paper bag.

Several days and nights went by, but nothing changed. The pills and ear plugs provided no relief. The days were not quite as long as the nights, because I was not alone. But they were bad enough.

Judy was loving and concerned, but beginning to worry. Each day when I came home, I spilled it all to her—the fear and the panic.

"Is there anything we're overlooking?" she would ask.

I sat and racked my brain. I searched into every corner of my existence. "There's nothing I know of."

"Maybe there's something causing your feelings that appears trivial," she suggested.

In deep frustration, I stomped around the room. "My

life is full of trivial problems, just like everyone else's!" I said. "If one of them is important, how would I know it?"

"There has to be something," she said.

"I *know* there has to be something."

"Come and sit down," she said. "Try to calm down."

I sat down next to her on the couch and clenched my fists. I was anything but calm. "I've gone over and over every part of my life. And every part of our life together. If there's anything at all that could be causing these feelings, I can't tell you what it is."

Then she said softly, "We're going over the same ground again and again."

"I know."

"All we're doing is repeating ourselves." She took my hand and held it.

"I know. I know."

"Maybe you'd better get some help. A counselor or something."

I had often thought the same thing but never dared to voice it. It made me feel inept to think I needed therapy. "I'm afraid to," I said.

"Why?"

"I'm afraid because I think there might be something seriously wrong with me."

"But maybe a counselor could help you figure it out."

"I know. Maybe."

Judy was frustrated and had done all the digging she knew how to do. "Maybe it will just go away," she said, squeezing my hand.

I felt a little better and looked at her. "Yeah, maybe you're right. It came all of a sudden, maybe it will disappear the same way. Maybe it will all blow over."

"Sure. We might as well look on the bright side. Sooner or later, it has to go away. It just has to."

I believed those words. I had lived thirty years as a

"normal" person. It had to go away. It had to go away, because now I was feeling worthless; I was filled with self-disgust. I was a freak. This madness had to go away.

It had to, but it didn't.

The next morning, I was feeling particularly wretched; my stomach began to tighten like a metal ball as I shaved. Jason came toddling into the bathroom and put up his hand for some shaving lather. I put a small dab on his fingers. Thrilled, he began to dab the lather on his face. I looked at him, standing there in an undershirt and rubber pants. His blond hair was soft and thin. In less than four weeks he would be a year old. He smiled broadly with the shaving lather on his face.

Instead of feeling joy at this precious moment, I felt fear and despair clawing at my insides; what if I fell apart and my little one was taken away from me? Inside, I wept at this disheartening juxtaposition: the joy that I *should* be feeling, looking at him, and cherishing him, next to the terror that I *was* feeling.

On the following morning as I brushed my teeth, I began to gag and vomit. I draped myself over the toilet, heaving dry heaves. I was appalled at my condition. On subsequent mornings, I feared brushing my teeth, afraid that if I did, I would vomit again.

A pattern began to take shape: each morning, the terror seized me. About mid-day, it reached its peak. By late afternoon and evening it began to abate and I felt a relative calm. At bedtime it seized me with such strength that I often wept.

On *Super Sunday*, in mid-January, we watched the Super Bowl game with friends in their home. I am a sports freak; I love to watch football games, bowl games in particular. But I could not concentrate. My stomach was knotted in fear, and I could not get absorbed in the game. The Dallas Cowboys were playing somebody, but all I saw was one group running from right to left, and the other group running the other way.

After the game, we had home-made pizza, which Ruth had prepared. I could not eat the supper.

"Don't you like the pizza?" asked Ruth.

"Oh yes, it's very good," I said.

"Pizza's one of your favorites, Jim."

"I'm afraid I'm coming down with something," I said. Then I decided to lie a little bit more: "I have a sore throat, and my stomach is bothering me."

"That's too bad."

I drank some Pepsi and let it go at that.

That night when we got home, I stepped on the bathroom scales. I had lost ten pounds in ten days; my weight had gone from 180 to 170. This scared me.

Often, I went out by myself into the fields near our house. I sat on the fieldstone fence to the west of the farmyard. I looked at our pretty stone house, built in 1780. To the north of it stood the landlord's stone house, much larger, also built of stone in the same period. To the south was another farmer's house, a green wooden two-story home. Behind me were wheat fields, rolling hills covered with snow, and to the east, across the road, a low mountain range, snow-covered and dotted with bare trees and evergreens.

Our house was so beautiful and so peaceful-looking, and so were the surroundings. Smoke was rising from the chimney, and I knew that to anyone who drove past, it would seem as if only peace and joy would dwell within. This thought angered me.

"This can't be happening!" I yelled at the top of my lungs. "Not to me!"

In desperation, I ordered God: "Take this away! This can't be happening to me!"

I cut firewood furiously by the hour with a bow saw until my right arm and shoulder ached. It seemed to offer a release. Still, I could find no cause for the terror; still, it did not diminish.

Each day, I forced myself to get going. Bewildered, I stayed on schedule, although I wanted to roll into a ball and cry and cry. I charged through my classes and my paper grading. At school, I hungered for social situations that would take my mind off my difficulties.

I loved to talk with Arthur, my fellow teacher and good friend. Arthur was eccentric and kind, and he loved to tell stories. So did I, and I loved to listen to the stories he told. Arthur had grown up in Jersey City, during the depression. One morning we were discussing desirable and undesirable cities in which to live. "There's this story that people from Jersey City often tell," he began. "It seems that God was feeling very angry with the people of Earth one day, and he sent two angels to Earth to investigate human wickedness, and to suggest an appropriate punishment. As it turned out, the two angels happened to alight in Jersey City, where they spent their afternoon. Later in the day, they returned to heaven and said to God, 'What we have seen on earth is so disgusting that there is no point in punishing people further; they are punished enough.' "

Another time we were discussing the coverage of sporting events on television. This led Arthur to recall his childhood. "There were barbershops and candy stores in Jersey City that used to keep people posted on World Series scores. The men in the store would listen to the Series game on the radio, and at the end of each inning they would use a crayon and write the score on a large piece of cardboard. They put the cardboard in the front window of the store, facing out, so that passers-by would know the score of the game. Each inning, the score would be brought up to date."

Arthur told such stories by the hour. He cherished the special little details of living that made life interesting. Listening to his stories was a pleasure and a release for me; for a few moments, I was transported away from my problems.

The first semester ended in the last week of January,

and I worked furiously, marking final examinations and doing end-of-the-term paper work. I found that keeping busy was a partial release; I could get absorbed in work. I graded the final exams and recorded all the grades in my grade book. I filled out other student reports, then typed them in triplicate and filed them in a special file, just to create extra busy work. I wanted the work to be as consuming as possible.

After all the paper work was done, I seized other furious activities to throw myself into. Judy and I planned a garden for spring, at least eight to ten weeks away. The garden-planning offered me an opportunity to follow Judy's leadership. She was interested not only in growing vegetables but also in freezing and canning. Further, she was and is good at planning projects carefully, in order to ensure their success.

I cut more and more firewood until my entire body ached. I would sit at the typewriter for hours, typing letters of introduction and application for teaching jobs in Europe. In this too, Judy and I worked together. We had spent a year in the western part of Ireland a few years previous, when I had taken a leave of absence from teaching to work on some writing. We had done some traveling at that time throughout Europe. We had both enjoyed that experience, but Judy especially had developed a special fondness for Irish culture and people. We both hoped that some day we could return to Ireland.

I realize now this typing was essentially busywork. I was so shaken by the terror I was experiencing that I was not really capable of evaluating my urge for a European teaching position; but the typing was absorbing.

In the evening, there were usually tears in my eyes as Jason and I played with building blocks and toy cars on the living room floor. I feared that my life, as I knew it, might be just about over. I might be ready to collapse. My career in education, my son, my dear wife, my friends—all might be torn away from me at any time.

One evening as I was playing with Jason on the floor, a

commercial came on television. I usually watched commercials because Jason did—they interested him more than the programming. In this commercial, a woman was embarrassed because she had age spots on her hands. Her friend acknowledged that this condition was indeed "heartbreaking," but then she recommended a medicated cream that would make the spots disappear. At the end of the commercial, the woman had used the cream successfully, and her age spots were gone.

I was furious at the ad. How dare these people whine about those petty problems? How *dare* they? "Who cares about age spots?" I asked out loud, angrily.

Judy looked at me, perplexed. "It's stupid!" I continued. "There are terrible problems in the world! Terrible ones! People are suffering and hurting and dying! Why should I care about this stupid woman's age spots?"

Judy didn't answer, obviously afraid she would only anger me more.

The next afternoon, I came home from school, typically shaken. I was still terrified and confused.

"Nanny's been gone all day," Judy announced.

Nanny was our dog, a large, gentle Labrador and Malamute mix. "It's not unusual for her to run off for a while," I said.

"But she's been gone all day. I haven't seen her once."

For some reason, my stomach constricted sharply with a sense of dread. I tried to throw it off: "Oh, she's probably out running in the timber. She'll be back, you'll see."

After supper, we called the dog several times, but there was no sign of her. Before we went to bed, Judy said, "I'm real worried about our doggie."

"I know."

"I'm just afraid something terrible has happened to her. There are people who steal dogs and sell them to labs for experiments."

I put my arms around her, feeling more fear than she,

but not wanting to show it. "She runs through the woods a lot. She'll probably come home during the night," I said.

I didn't believe it though, and spent another long and fearful night. I worried about the dog. I worried that she was dead on the road somewhere. The intensity of my fear was devastating; I was unable to handle this problem.

The next morning at breakfast, I was exhausted and my eyes burned as usual. I cut up Jason's toast in little squares; it was a favorite game of ours. I looked out the front window; out of a dull gray sky, a fine snow was blowing.

Judy came back into the house from calling the dog. She shook her head without speaking.

Without appetite, I nibbled a little breakfast and then headed for school. I finished my grade cards and turned them in. The semester was over.

By lunchtime, there was a blizzard. The heavy snow was blowing horizontally. I was worried about the dog and called Judy at home. There was still no sign of her. I felt an especially disproportionate dread about the dog's absence, and my overreaction disheartened me.

I drove home at three o'clock through the blizzard, moving at only twenty miles per hour. The road was scarcely visible. When I arrived, Judy was very discouraged. "Still no dog," she said sadly.

"What do you suppose has happened to her?" I asked.

"I don't know, it could be anything. Oh, I feel so bad! She's out there in this blizzard. She could be hurt on the road somewhere, or even shot. I hope she's not suffering." She was trying not to cry.

I felt an enormous panic inside. It was as if my nameless fears had grasped this event hungrily, in order to have a target. I went out into the field behind our house and then into the farmyard. I called and called the dog, and I whistled several times. No luck.

When I went back into the house, Judy said, "I called

the radio station and the humane society to report her missing."

I nodded.

"I doubt if it will do any good, but I had to do something."

After supper, I felt more desperate about the dog, and more helpless. I had to go and look for her.

"I've got to go look for her," I said. I got my boots and coat.

"Not now, Jim—not in this blizzard."

"I've got to," I said.

"It's not safe to be out in this; don't go."

"I just have to," I said again. My insides were churning.

"Please don't," Judy said. She was afraid.

"I'll be back soon," I said, heading out the door.

The thermometer by our front door read eight degrees above zero. The wind was howling out of the northwest, and the snow cut at my face like a blade. I started down the road, walking south. The snow was getting deep; the road had not been plowed, and with this wind, plowing would be pointless anyway. Occasionally, there were tire tracks in the snow.

I walked two miles to the south, calling at each of the six farmhouses I passed on the way. There was no sign of our dog.

I went about half a mile along the road to the west, and I felt like my body was frozen. I decided to head back to the north through the woods, even though I knew it was a wrong decision. In the woods, the wind was almost as strong as it had been out on the road. I called and called for the dog, desperately, knowing deep inside it was futile.

Much deeper into the woods, I suddenly realized I might freeze to death here. My hands and face ached with the cold. Snow had worked down inside of my boots; my feet were wet and freezing. I decided I must get back up to the road.

I headed back in the direction I assumed was east. I was seized with a terrible panic: I might not make it. I knew about frostbite and hypothermia, and I knew that I could freeze to death. If I was not headed due east, I could be in the woods too long and might not have time to make it home.

The wind cut at my face painfully. My body was sluggish as I sunk deeply into the snow with every step. Small tree branches frequently whipped me in the face, and I began to sob desperately.

I slipped and fell at one point; my right knee slammed heavily on top of a large rock. A sharp pain shot through my right leg; hysterically, I began to sob. The fact that I was now in a predicament that threatened my life was squarely before me. All the fears and terrors of those many days swept over me, and I trembled with panic. I wondered if I had come out here to die—was this a form of suicide? I cried desperately; I did not want to die. I knew I wasn't going to find the dog. I wanted to get home and sort out my life.

I got up and stumbled on. My right knee ached sharply and could not support much weight. I sobbed and moved on.

Then I saw the road. I crossed the ditch, climbed up on the road, and headed north. The icy wind was now directly in my face, and I still had a mile and a half to go. It seemed to take the rest of the night, but somehow, I finally managed to get home. Parts of my body ached with a terrible agony, and other parts were numb.

I stumbled into the house. Judy was white with panic. "I was terrified," she said, beginning to cry. "I even called the state police."

The late news was on. It stunned me to realize I had been out for nearly four hours.

My fingers were not functional. Judy had to unbutton my coat and pull off my boots. She ran a dishpan of lukewarm water and then pulled off my socks, which were wet and partially frozen. I sat in front of the fireplace and put my feet into the water; I held my hands close to the fire. I was shaking and felt like my body was on fire. I felt not only a physical misery, but I was devastated by my terror and irrational behavior.

Judy was still crying. "I was terrified," she said again.

My fingers and toes were frostbitten. For several years, those parts of my body would cause me discomfort. We did not see the dog again; after two weeks, we finally resigned ourselves to the fact the dog was gone permanently.

On the day following my dog-search episode, I was driving home late in the afternoon from a department meeting. Happening to remember that Judy wanted a digital clock radio, I stopped at Black's, a large chain-store discount house that was going out of business.

Inside, the huge store had the dislocated, out-of-joint climate of a business that is selling merchandise, but not replenishing any. Most of the shelves were empty or nearly-empty. I went to the small appliance counter, and they had the kind of clock radio we wanted; it was on sale for twenty dollars, barely half of its suggested price. The sales clerk set it on the counter and I stared at it. As I did so, my stomach contracted with fear. I felt that if I bought the radio, I was somehow affirming the fact that I could continue living as a normal person; I had no confidence whatsoever that such a future lay before me.

I looked at the radio and began to panic and sweat.

"Well?" said the sales clerk impatiently.

It was nearly impossible for me to decide. The radio represented normalcy, and I did not feel like normalcy was part of my future.

Finally, in a panic, I bought the radio and hurried to the car. There were tears in my eyes. In the dark, I drove home.

When I got home, Judy was watching the six o'clock news on television. I went upstairs to the bathroom and weighed myself. I had lost two more pounds, down to 168. I shook my head.

I went into Jason's bedroom and looked at him, sleeping in his crib. I pulled up his covers, even though they didn't need pulling up. He was sleeping blissfully and I watched him for several moments. Then, slowly and quietly, I began to cry. The tears ran down my cheeks and into my mouth. I thought again of the radio. Three weeks had passed, and I was still the same wretched man. Nothing had changed.

Still crying, I went downstairs. Judy came to me and put her arms around me. I cried and cried.

We sat together on the couch. "I need help," I said.

"I know," she said, holding me close.

"I need help," I repeated. "I can't go on like this."

"O.K., we'll get some help. It's the right thing."

"I can't believe I'm saying this," I sobbed.

"It's good that you are. Maybe it's the first step toward getting well."

There I was, finally, staring face to face at an utterly shocking reality: I could not continue my own life on my own resources. A person's life *can suddenly go out of control.* And it wasn't just something that happened to other people. It was happening to me.

Two

*T*he only person I could think of to go to for help was a man I had gotten to know some months earlier. He was an ex-Baptist minister who was currently working as a counselor in a multi-purpose counseling center. His name was Dick Dutton.

I wasn't really enthused about seeing a Baptist minister. To begin with, I had not been involved in the Christian life, or in any kind of church life, for some years. In addition, I had been raised in a Methodist parsonage; our style of religion had always been polite, dignified, and for the most part, private. In my mind, the words "Baptist minister" signified fire and brimstone and shouted hallelujahs.

Furthermore, this particular counseling center, as I understood it, was primarily for drug rehabilitation and for families of those with drug problems. But I was desperate, and I had nowhere else to turn.

So I called him up. In just a sentence or two, I summarized what I had been going through. I must have sounded pretty desperate, because he said, "You'd better come right over."

His office was located in an old, two-story frame house in need of paint. I met Dick in the front room, which must have been the office for everyone who worked there; there were three desks, a secretary's table, and a mimeograph machine in a room not much larger than twelve by fifteen feet. There were papers and materials and books piled everywhere. Dick met me and shook my hand. "Come in, Jim; let's go into the conference room."

The conference room was a converted back porch. There was unpainted sheet rock covering some of the windows, and the only furniture consisted of a small wooden table with a straight chair, a torn couch, and an overstuffed chair with a matching tear.

"Sit down," said Dick. He motioned at the room and at the building in general. "We're trying to get this place cleaned up and remodeled. This center is new, and we're on a very limited budget."

We sat down. Dick Dutton was forty-two years old, but he looked younger. He was rugged, lean, and muscular. He wore blue jeans and a V-neck, pale blue sweater.

He said, "You sounded pretty desperate on the phone. What's happening with you?"

I looked around briefly at the bare room. The ramshackle condition of the building did not give me any confidence, but I didn't hold anything back. I spilled it all to him. I just poured it out—the fear, the panic, the disorientation—the lack of any apparent cause. I remember how good it felt just to unload on somebody. Before I got finished, I started to cry, with a mild sense of relief.

Dick listened with compassion. He reached over and put his hand on the back of my hands. His hands were clean, but large and rough and split, like carpenter's hands. "Something has to be causing your feelings," he said. "We just have to figure out what."

I got out my handkerchief and blew my nose. I was ashamed to be seen crying.

"Has anything like this ever happened to you before?" he asked.

"No. Never."

"Have you never been scared before?"

"Oh yes; but I always knew what I was afraid of. I could identify the cause of the fear. I've never been scared of nothing before."

"Oh, there's probably something. We just don't know what it is."

"Could be," I said, but I was unconvinced. I had gone over it too many times in my mind.

"Are you a tense person?"

I had to think for a moment. "Yes, I suppose so."

"Do you tend to worry about things?"

"Yes, I do. But I've never felt anything like this before."

"You say there's nothing unusual going on in your life at all?"

I shook my head. "No. Nothing. There's nothing happening in my life that's scary, or even unusual."

"Would you tell me if there was?"

I looked at him. He was smiling. I liked and trusted him. "Yes, I would. I can't go on with these feelings. I have to get to the bottom of this."

"What were you doing just before these feelings began?"

"We were back in Illinois for Christmas, visiting my parents and my wife's parents."

"How did the visit go?"

"Fine. It went fine."

"Are you lonely for your parents? Is your wife lonely for her parents?"

"I don't think so; not especially. We have a son now,

and we both wish we could get him together with his grandparents more often. This was the first time we had ever taken
him to Illinois for a visit."

"Maybe that's important," he suggested.

I began to feel frustration creeping in. I shrugged my
shoulders: "Maybe it is; I don't know."

"Are you feeling frustrated?"

"Yes, I am. I could go on and on. Maybe this is important, maybe that is important. Maybe something else is important, maybe nothing is important. How would I know?" I
was also feeling discouraged. I turned to him and asked, "Do
you know what's going on with me?"

He shook his head quickly. "No, I don't. There's something going on, but I couldn't guess what."

This bothered me a little. I guess I expected an instant
answer. I had told him the problem, now it was his turn to
provide the answer.

Dick stood up. "I'll tell you what," he said. "We have a
psychiatrist who is with us one day a week. It so happens that
he's here today. I'd like you to talk with him. Would you be
willing to do that?"

"Sure," I said.

Dick went to get him. My spirits soared when I realized
I would get to talk with a psychiatrist. Here would be an
answer, I thought.

Dick brought the psychiatrist in. He was Irish, and his
name was Dr. O'Mahoney. He shook hands with me, then he
sat on the straight chair and pulled up to the small table. He
was very fat, and had thinning, oily hair. He had a full black
beard and a very round face. The starched collar of his white
dress shirt cut into his fat neck. He folded his hands on the table; he wore several rings on his pudgy fingers.

Dr. O'Mahoney spoke in a thick brogue, and we had
trouble communicating. He asked me to tell about my feel-

ings. I went over it all in a rush, describing briefly the fear and the panic. He asked me about our trip to Illinois at Christmas. He asked me about our families: "How do you get along with your father and your mother?"

"I get along fine with my mother."

"And your father?"

"Well, we have some problems now and then. We get into quarrels a good deal of the time."

"What kind of quarrels?"

I had to think a moment. "I'm not sure."

"What kind of quarrels?" he repeated. His eyes were closed, his hands still clasped.

I felt under pressure. "I'm not sure I could explain the quarrels very well. I guess it's that he always wanted me to do chores or tasks his way, and I always wanted the chance to do things my own way." Saying this, I felt foolish; this was the distant past, mostly. Where would it get us?

"How old are you?"

"Thirty-two," I said.

Dr. O'Mahoney closed his eyes again and asked another question: "How long have you been having these kinds of quarrels with your father?"

I shrugged. "Ever since high school, I guess. Maybe longer."

He nodded. "How is your father's health?"

"Well, O.K., I guess. He's had heart attacks."

"How many heart attacks?"

"Two or three, I guess." I felt frightened, and I didn't feel like this was getting us anywhere.

He asked me another question: "Have you ever had feelings like this before?"

"No. Never."

He nodded his head, straightened his tie, and then re-clasped his hands. "I will summarize now. Here is what I believe is taking place. You have much anger at your father. You believe he has betrayed you by neglecting you. Now you are afraid he might die soon, and you are full of guilt. You are afraid he will die while you still hold these feelings of anger towards him."

I didn't know what to say. I remember saying to him, "That's very Freudian, isn't it?"

"Yes, it is," he said. "It is also very true."

I asked him how he could figure it all out so fast. Didn't he need more information?

"I have seen hundreds of cases like yours," he responded. "Hundreds. You are having an acute anxiety attack. You need medicine to calm you down, and then you need psychotherapy."

"For how long?" I blurted out. "I want to get over this."

"Who knows? These things take time."

"What did you say I was having?"

"An acute anxiety attack." Then he repeated, "There are medicines that can calm you down, then you need psychotherapy."

"Who would give me the therapy?"

"That is up to you," he shrugged.

Dick had not spoken at all. Now, he asked a question: "Dr. O'Mahoney, are you recommending psychotherapy as the best course for Jim to take?"

"That is the best course." Dr. O'Mahoney stood up. "Now if you will excuse me." He stood to leave.

"Thank you for your time," Dick said as he left.

"Thank you," I murmured. I felt utterly despondent. There was my fast answer: *acute anxiety attack*. It sounded so trivial, like the temporary apprehension of calling up a girl for a date. For feelings that were tearing at my guts, it just wasn't adequate. But I had my fast answer, and I certainly didn't like it.

Furthermore, extended psychotherapy meant that it could be weeks before I shook off these feelings.

Or months.

Or years.

Or never.

Dick was apologetic. "These psychiatrists are very busy; they often get in a hurry."

"Yes, I understand," I murmured. Dr. O'Mahoney's abruptness had frightened me. I was not inclined to accept his analysis, accurate as it may have been.

"What he said may give us something to work on, though."

I turned to look at him. Now I had tears blurring my eyes again. "I wouldn't know where to go for therapy," I said.

"I can help you with that if you'd like me to."

"I just don't know," I said.

"Does it scare you? Therapy?"

"Yes, it does," I answered quickly.

"Don't let it scare you." He put his hand on mine again. "Don't decide now. Think it over."

I shook my head, not wanting to speak for fear I would cry.

"Talk it over with Judy. Think it over. Call me up if you want to talk. I'll help you in any way I can."

Before I left, I shook hands with Dick and thanked him. He was trying to soothe me, but I was not soothed. If anything, my fears were greater than before. Talking with Dr. O'Mahoney had scared me: I felt like I had something terribly wrong with me, which would take a long, long time to straighten out.

I drove home, panicky and confused. Dick Dutton had been as mystified as I was, and I felt Dr. O'Mahoney had given me the bum's rush. My first contact with the world of therapy was not encouraging.

"How did it go?" Judy asked me when I got home.

"I don't know. I don't know if we got anywhere. I'm confused."

"Did you get to talk to Dick?"

"Yes, I talked to him, and then I talked to this psychiatrist named Dr. O'Mahoney."

"What was it like talking to him?"

I made a face and waved my hand in dismissal. "He was in a hurry. I don't think he cared about what I was telling him."

"Don't be negative," she said. "The problem may be complicated, it might take time to sort it out." I knew she was afraid and wanted only to be encouraging.

"I'm afraid you're right about that." I felt only discouragement. I didn't know if counseling or therapy would do me any good.

"What did they ask you about?" she said.

"I'll tell you in a minute." I went upstairs and changed into old clothes—blue jeans and a flannel shirt. I weighed myself. 166. I stopped for a moment in Jason's room, where he was napping. For some moments, I watched him sleeping. I felt an ache inside.

I went back downstairs and sat at the kitchen table with Judy. "Dick Dutton and Dr. O'Mahoney were interested in our trip to Illinois at Christmas. They wanted to know how I felt about my parents and about your parents. They wanted to know if there was any conflict during the visit."

"You had a couple of arguments with your father."

"Don't I always? That's nothing new."

"What were you arguing with him about?"

"Oh, I don't know; there's always something."

"No, tell me. What did you argue with him about?"

I buried my face in my hands. I tried to remain calm, and I tried to remember the arguments. "One was about

George McGovern," I said. "And another was about Richard Nixon."

"Politics?"

I still had my face in my hands. "Yes, well, that was the issue that got the argument *started*. You know, we always find a pretext for having an argument; then after that, it's a question of power—who's right, who's wrong, who's going to back down, who's going to win."

"You don't think it's important then?"

"No, I don't. I've been arguing with my father for years. It's nothing new. You know I've had conflicts with my father since junior high school."

"Still, it might be important, if Dick and the psychiatrist think so."

Now I felt frustration gnawing away inside me. "Anything might be important," I declared. "I can't tell what's going on. Anything might be important. I just don't know."

"Are you going to see Dick again?"

"I don't know. My experience today didn't give me much hope."

"I wish you'd see him again; give it some time."

I put my face in my hands again. I thought about the nights of naked terror and the days of mystifying panic. "Maybe I will." I felt truly helpless. "Maybe I will, I don't know."

Before I went to bed that night, I pulled out all the psychology books I had accumulated over the years. I needed to understand what acute anxiety was. By combining pieces and elements from the different books, I was able to form a definition I thought I could understand.

Anxiety is distinct from *fear* in that fear derives from an identifiable cause or threat, while anxiety does not. People with anxiety suffer the symptoms of fear, but without any apparent cause.

The more precise condition that was afflicting me is often labeled "generalized" anxiety, or "free-floating" anxiety. A person who suffers from generalized anxiety has chronic, persistent symptoms of panic and apprehensiveness, but those symptoms do not stem from any cause that can be identified. At some times the feelings of apprehensiveness are more acute than at others, but they are nearly always present. The physiological symptoms of panic are a part of generalized anxiety. Symptoms such as rapid pulse, elevated blood pressure, clamminess, and insomnia are common.

I found also in my reading that sufferers of generalized anxiety disorder often live for many years in chronic, apprehensive discomfort, although they usually do not lose their grip of reality, and they are usually able to function.

Knowing this information did not help me at all; I was terrified by it.

The next day, and the one following, Judy and I reconstructed many parts of our trip to Illinois, looking for clues. We did not seem to get anywhere.

I tried willing my feelings away. "Get out!" I commanded. I had a talk with myself, telling myself that with a power of will, I could force my feelings of terror to disappear. It was just a matter of will power.

I went around the house with false good humor, laughing and telling jokes. I told Judy the story Arthur had told me about the angels coming to visit Jersey City. She smiled politely. I read her the comics from the newspaper, and the answers "Dear Abby" gave to her letter-writers. I laughed out loud, with false humor.

I tossed Jason up and down, "Wheeeeeboy!" I yelled. "Wheeeeeboy! Let's go shopping!"

It was a miserable failure. Nothing was funny, nor did it feel funny. I felt pitiful.

The following day, I went to bed in the middle of the day

and curled myself into a ball. "This can't be happening; this can't be happening," I repeated over and over.

It was happening.

Late that afternoon I called Dick Dutton again on the phone. I was weeping; I told him how desperate everything was. I told him I didn't think I could survive what was happening. He invited me right over.

We sat in the conference room again. "How bad are you hurting?" he asked.

It was very hard for me to explain my feelings to anyone. Nobody seemed to be able to relate to the experience. "Dick, remember the time in your life when you were most terrified of something? Have you ever been just shaking with panic? If you have, remember what it felt like."

"O.K. I'm with you."

"Now, imagine that you have all those feelings of terror, but no cause for them. There's nothing happening in your life to cause your terror, yet you still have it."

"That would be scary," he nodded. "Would you like some coffee?"

"I couldn't drink another cup. Thanks anyway."

"Jim, I don't know what's going on with you. I'll be honest. I think you need more expertise than I've got. I'd like to see you go for some therapy at County Mental Health."

I felt devastated. I looked down and picked at my fingernails. I liked and trusted Dick; I wanted him to solve my problem.

"I know you're disappointed," he said softly.

I still looked down. "I'm afraid there's something really wrong with me," I said. To avoid crying, I didn't say anymore.

He walked over and put his hand on my shoulder. I was so grateful to him for doing that; I loved him deeply at that moment. He went on softly, "Let me call the mental health unit. Let me see how to get you started there. I don't think you'll be spending the rest of your life there, but maybe you can get started on something helpful."

I couldn't speak; I simply nodded my head up and down. I sat there as he phoned the county mental health unit to see how I could be admitted to the hospital. My stomach knotted up.

Dick hung up the phone. "To be admitted to the mental health unit, you need to go through the hospital emergency room," he said. "It's just a procedure you go through. Why don't you go right over—they're expecting you."

I was stunned. Dick left the conference room so that I could use the phone in privacy. I called Judy and told her what I was doing. She did not answer, and I knew she was crying. Finally, she said, "Maybe it's the best thing."

"I don't know," I said.

"Maybe it's the best thing," she repeated. "You owe it to yourself."

"I just don't know." I hung up and drove to the county hospital in a neighboring town.

The hospital was a new brick building, low and long with lots of glass. I went in through the emergency entrance and spoke to a receptionist behind a glass partition. I gave her my name.

"What can we do for you?"

"Dick Dutton called you. He told you I was coming."

"Who's Dick Dutton?"

I felt my insides seizing up. "He's a counselor for PATH; he called to tell you I was coming."

"Who did he talk to, do you know?" She was young, but wore lots of makeup, and her black hair was stiff with hairspray.

"No, I don't know," I snapped.

The receptionist turned to a nurse who was seated at a

nearby desk, looking through some folders. "Did you take a call from someone named Dick Dutton?"

"No," said the nurse, without looking up.

The receptionist turned back to me, with no change of expression on her face. "What kind of problem are you having?"

I was feeling very panicky. I had an urge to smash the glass partition with my fists. "It's not something I want to talk to you about. It's emotional. I'm supposed to see a therapist."

She took out a white form. "Name?"

I proceeded to tell her my name, age, address, place of employment, and telephone number.

"Insurance?" she asked.

"What do you mean?"

"Insurance. Who do you have your insurance with?"

"I don't know. I teach at the college; whoever they have it with."

"Do you have an insurance identification card?"

I was feeling tighter and tighter. "No, I don't." I took out my wallet and gave her my faculty identification card. "There; maybe that will help."

She examined the card and wrote something more on the form. "Wait in the second room on your right. Someone will be in to see you."

"What?"

She repeated the instructions, and I went to the second room on the right, which turned out to be a medical examining room. Wretched, I sat on the edge of the examining table. There were cabinets of first-aid items, an eye chart, blood pressure cuff, and other standard items. The light was very bright.

I sat by myself for several minutes. I could not accept the fact that I was here.

The longer I sat by myself, the greater were my feelings

of panic and humiliation. I decided I would count to ten, and if no one came by that time, I would simply get up and walk out. I counted very slowly from one to ten, and then, miserably, decided to do it again.

Finally, two women came in and sat down. The first was young and attractive, with dark hair and large glasses with dark frames. She put out her hand, "Hi, I'm Sarah. This is DeeAnn. We're both here to help you if we can." I shook hands with both of them. DeeAnn was older. She was large and chubby, with short red hair.

Sarah explained that they were both social workers, employed full-time by the mental health unit. She asked me my name, and then she asked me to talk about myself and my feelings.

They both took notes as I told them my story. By now, I was getting used to telling it.

"Jim, have you ever had these kind of panicky feelings before?" asked Sarah.

"Not without a cause," I said.

"Not without a cause you can identify," she corrected.

"O.K., all right."

"How is your health?"

"My health is fine."

"Have you had a physical examination lately?"

"No."

"Have you had any illness recently?"

"I've had a cold. That's all."

DeeAnn was asking some of the questions.

"Have you had any head injury recently? Or blow to the head?"

"No."

"Are you presently on any medication?"

"No."

"Do you use drugs of any kind?"

"No."

"Not ever?"

"No."

"Do you smoke marijuana?"

"No, I don't smoke marijuana."

Then Sarah put away her notebook. She looked straight into my eyes. "Jim, why do you think you need therapy? What do you think we can do to help you?"

I was confused. I thought it should be obvious. "I need an answer," I said. "I need to know what's happening to me."

"Why?"

"I can't go on like this; I can't live like this."

"Do you think we can help you?"

"I don't know. I don't know anything about therapy."

Then DeeAnn and Sarah took me down the hallway, out of the main hospital and into the mental health unit. The building was new, with gold carpeting and a comfortable lounge on both the first and second floors. I looked into one of the resident rooms. It was a pleasant room with twin beds and beige bedspreads. It looked warm and inviting.

There were no locks on any of the doors and no bars on any of the windows. I realized that people could come and go as they chose.

The three of us sat down on a comfortable couch in the second floor lounge. In the corner, two men were watching television. The walls were painted with pastel colors—mostly beige and pale blue.

"We're not going to recommend that you be a resident here," said Sarah.

Without speaking, I looked down. I felt afraid, and I felt too timid to voice any opinions.

"We're going to recommend that you come each day for therapy but that you operate strictly on an outpatient basis."

To my amazement, I was disappointed. When I saw the hospital, I just wanted to curl up inside it and have the staff chase all my problems away. The thought that had terrified me more than any other was the possible separation from my family. Yet here I was, longing to curl up inside the hospital.

"Why?" I asked. "Why only as an outpatient?"

DeeAnn answered. "If you can possibly function on the outside, we want you to do it. It's always the best way."

I think Sarah sensed my disappointment and confusion. "We think you should come each day and spend the whole day," she said. "From eight in the morning till five in the afternoon. But we also want you hanging in there, on the outside."

I drove home in disbelief, still repeating: "This can't be happening." Tomorrow morning, I would be a mental patient.

Later that evening, Judy and I went to see George and Eva, my department chairman and his wife. They had a luxurious older home, finely furnished. Eva poured everybody a sherry in cut crystal glasses.

I told them what was happening to me. I felt angry and humiliated that I had to disclose all of this to yet another set of people. I felt ashamed and worthless, like a freak who couldn't handle the simple business of living.

They were both shocked to hear I was having these problems. "You, of all people!" exclaimed Eva. "You are always so composed!"

"It sounds like you're having a rough time of it," said George.

"Of all the people," said Eva. "You would be the last I would expect to have such a problem." She clucked her tongue.

I told them I would be entering therapy, and I might not be able to start the second semester on time.

"Take all the time you need," said George.

"What about registration?" I asked.

"Don't worry about it. Registration can get along just fine without you."

I was grateful to him.

"As far as I'm concerned," he went on, "you have no real obligation at the college until February 12. That's the first day of classes, if my memory serves me."

"Thanks a lot, George, I appreciate your help." Today was February 1. I had nearly two weeks without job responsibility.

"Not at all."

Then Eva spoke up: "Therapy will not do any good," she declared bluntly. "Medication is the only answer. If you want to get well, get the right medication."

This declaration scared me. "Eva, I'm going to start therapy the first thing tomorrow morning; I have to have some faith in it."

"I'm not trying to destroy your faith. I'm trying to help you. I've had some experience with anxiety and tension. Medication is the answer."

I remember how I had often observed Eva to be drowsy, and now I understood that the drowsiness was probably caused by medication. She used medication, and it made her feel better. But I was revolted by the thought of medication; it seemed to me like a cop-out and an admission of failure, although I don't know why.

I could only repeat to her, "If I'm going to start with therapy, I have to believe in it. I have to believe in *something*."

Three

*T*he next morning, early, I drove to the hospital. The sun was rising on a clear blue sky and fields covered with snow. As I drove, I felt tense and apprehensive, and my mind was filled with questions. What was a mental hospital like? What kinds of people would be there? Would there be violent people? Would there be anyone there with a problem like mine? And most of all, I wondered if this process was going to help me.

When I got to the hospital, Sarah met me and took me upstairs to the second floor lounge. "Your therapy group meets here," she said. "Just get a cup of coffee and make yourself at home; we won't be starting for a few minutes."

There were several people seated, drinking coffee. There was very little conversation. There was a "Sylvester and Tweety" cartoon on the television in the corner. Several people were watching it.

I sat down after pouring myself a cup of coffee. There were large windows in the lounge, and the sun glared in my eyes through a large east window.

DeeAnn and Sarah were talking next to the coffee pot.

They were looking inside a manilla folder. Two women in blue jeans came into the lounge and sat down next to each other.

Finally, a man wearing a blue sportcoat and a striped tie got up and shut off the television set. The man was in his thirties; he was short and stocky, and he had black hair neatly combed. On his right hand was a large gold ring with a large diamond.

He sat down next to me. "Why don't we get started?" he said to the group.

"Let's don't and say we did," said a young man in the corner. Several people laughed. One young girl with long blond hair laughed a good deal.

The man in the sportcoat repeated himself: "Let's get started. We have two new people with us today. Let's all try to make them feel welcome."

He turned to me. "My name is Roger," he said. "Why don't you introduce yourself to the group."

"My name is Jim," I said. Nobody seemed to pay any attention. I was nervous. Several people were lighting up cigarettes.

"Let's all try to make Jim feel welcome," said Roger to the group. Then he turned to a woman sitting near his left. "Would you like to introduce yourself?"

The woman was young and attractive, probably in her late twenties. She had long black hair, and she wore a stylish beige pants suit. "My name is Vicky," she said, looking at her lap.

"We're glad you're with us, Vicky, and we hope that this group will be helpful to you." Then Roger turned to the rest of the group. "Why don't we go around the room and introduce ourselves to Jim and Vicky? And when you introduce yourself, explain briefly why you're here and what you're trying to deal with."

Roger paused to light a cigarette. He used a gold cigarette lighter. "Let's start on that side, shall we? Norman, why don't you go first?"

Norman looked down and fidgeted with his fingers. He had a round face and long blond hair that hung in his eyes. He was about twenty. "My name is Norman," he said.

"Speak up!" Sarah commanded.

I started in my chair; my heartbeat got suddenly rapid.

"My name is Norman," said Norman, a bit louder.

"And why are you here?" asked Roger.

"I don't know."

"Yes, you do. Why are you here?"

"I don't know how to handle authority," he mumbled.

"Speak up," Sarah repeated firmly. "Speak up and look up. Lift up your head when you speak. Look at me."

Norman looked up, red in the face, and said loudly, "I don't know how to handle authority."

"That's better," said Roger. "Next."

"My name is Louise," said a middle-aged woman to Norman's left. Louise had gray hair and was neatly dressed in a skirt and sweater.

"And why are you here?"

Without warning, Louise began to cry. She cried silently and dabbed at her eyes with a Kleenex.

"Why are you here?" insisted Sarah.

She did not answer, but went on crying.

"Louise, stop crying," said Sarah, "And tell us why you are here. Right now."

Louise blubbered through her tears: "I'm depressed. I went through the menopause, and now I'm depressed."

"And what are you doing about it, Louise? Stop crying and look up."

She looked up, but did not stop crying. "I'm learning self-respect."

"Then stop crying," said Roger. "Next."

Next was Diane. She was fifteen. She was very attractive, with straight blond hair, long enough that it rested on her
shoulders. She wore a wine-colored V-neck sweater and
clean blue jeans. "My name is Diane," she said. When she
spoke, she smiled.

"And why are you here, Diane?" asked DeeAnn. It was
the first time that DeeAnn had spoken.

"I'm into drugs."

"Let's hear it for dope!" declared Norman, and he
clapped his hands. Several people giggled.

"Ignore him," said Sarah. "Diane, why are you here?"

"I'm into drugs," said Diane. "I'm into acid, speed,
grass, any pill that I can get. Is that it?" She was smiling all the
while.

"No, that is not it," said Roger sternly. "Why are you
here?"

"I have hallucinations. I see little people. I've seen little
people walking on my body. Is that it?"

All of a sudden Vicky, the woman who was here for the
first time, began to cry. Roger looked at her briefly, then
turned back to Diane. "I'm going to give you one more
chance. If you get it wrong again, you lose TV time. Do you
hear me?"

Diane looked down. She was no longer smiling. "I
don't know how to make choices."

"Speak up!" said Sarah. "Speak up and look up!"

Diane looked up. Her eyes were glistening with tears. "I
can't make decisions."

"Why not?" demanded Sarah. "And speak up."

"I can't make choices because I let other people do it for
me," answered Diane.

"Better," said Roger. He turned to Vicky, who was still
sobbing. He passed her a Kleenex box.

"Thank you," she choked out.

"Did Diane say something that got to you?" asked Roger.

Vicky was too much out of control to speak, but she nodded her head up and down.

"Would you like to tell us about it?"

It took several moments for Vicky to compose herself enough to speak. "When she said something about hallucinations, it scared me."

"Why?" asked Sarah.

"I've been hearing voices."

"What kinds of voices?"

"Voices in the house. I've been hearing these voices in the house!" Then she broke down and sobbed horribly.

It took several moments for her to compose herself again, and then DeeAnn asked her, "Why don't you tell us a little bit about yourself, Vicky?"

"O.K."

"Where you're from, your family, things like that."

"O.K. We moved up here from Long Island about a month ago."

"Where is 'up here'? Do you mean here in town?"

Vicky nodded her head up and down. "We moved up here and bought a new house."

"Why did you move?" asked Roger.

"My husband got transferred."

"Were you happy to make the move?"

Vicky shook her head from side to side. She wiped her eyes and blew her nose. "No, I didn't want to move, but it was necessary for my husband's career." Then, suddenly, she began to sob again, and through her sobs she said, "I shouldn't even be here! I should be at home with my baby!"

"Why?" asked Sarah. "Are you letting your family down?"

"Yes."

"Tell us about your baby."

"His name is Jeremy."

"How old is he?"

"He's four. He's four years old."

"Then he's not really a baby at all, is he?" asked Sarah quietly.

"He's my baby!"

"A four-year-old is not a baby. You can see that, can't you?"

"I shouldn't even be here," Vicky repeated, sobbing.

Roger lit another cigarette and then asked Vicky, "Why don't you tell us about the voices?"

"I can't."

"Yes, you can. Tell us about the voices."

"It's the house! The new house is speaking to me with voices!"

"What are the voices like?" asked Sarah.

"The voices are telling me to go away."

"Go away from the house, you mean?"

"Yes. They're telling me to go away from the house!" Then Vicky broke down in pitiful sobbing. Through her sobs, she wailed, "Oh, this is horrible! Now you'll all think I'm even more whacked out than I am!" Her entire body was shaking.

These people were terrifying me. As Vicky spoke of her baby, I thought of Jason and how much I feared being separated from him.

Roger took a thoughtful puff on his cigarette and turned to Vicky once more. "Let's let it go for right now, Vicky, O.K.? You've given us all something to think about. Maybe this afternoon we'll come back to it." His voice was soothing, and Vicky nodded her head.

The hour was getting on; the only people left who had not spoken were myself, and the two women in blue jeans on the opposite couch. They were both masculine looking. They had short brown hair. They wore short-sleeved sport shirts and faded blue jeans. One of the women wore cowboy boots.

Roger turned to the two women. "Jessica, introduce yourself and introduce Jeanette. Tell us why you're here."

Jessica had a lot of acne on her face. When she spoke, she kept her face down and mumbled, so that she could not be heard.

"Speak up!" commanded Sarah. "Look up. Why are you here?"

"Me and Jeanette tried to kill ourselves."

"How?"

"We went in the linen closet and took pills together."

"What kind of pills?"

"I don't know."

"Speak up. Look up."

"I don't know what kind of pills!"

"That's not very bright, is it?" asked Roger. "Anyway, that's not why you're here. You took the pills after you came here. Why are you here?"

"I have some problems," she mumbled.

"Don't mumble."

"I have some problems."

"What problems do you have?"

"Sex," she said quietly, looking down. "I have sex problems."

"Jessica," asked Sarah, "what is your problem? Does it have a name?"

"I don't want to say," she said.

"Then I'll say it for you," Sarah continued. "You're a homosexual. Am I right?"

"I guess so," Jessica mumbled.

"Don't mumble. Am I right? Say it."

Jessica said something, too softly to be heard.

"Speak up."

"All right! I'm a homosexual!"

"Better. Do you like being a homosexual?"

"No!"

"Then you better do something about it," said Roger. "How about you, Jeanette?"

"I'm the same. I'm the same as Jesse."

"Which is?"

"A homosexual. I'm a homosexual." Her Adam's apple bounced up and down when she spoke.

"Do you like it?"

"I don't know."

"Then you'd better decide. Do you hear me? You'd better decide."

We were running out of time, and Roger turned to me. "Jim, would you like to tell the group briefly about what's been happening in your life?"

I looked around the circle. I felt panicky; these were crazy people. What was I doing here? What did they know? Why should I tell them anything? I didn't know how to begin. My mouth was dry.

As best as I could, I summarized what I had been going through.

Only the three therapists showed any interest. The members of the group looked bored. They had their heads down. The sunlight was glaring in my eyes, and the room was full of bluish cigarette haze.

When I finished summarizing, Roger said to the group: "Well, does anyone have a question? Can anyone help Jim?"

Nobody said anything. I felt very embarrassed. One feels, in any group, the need for acceptance, and I felt none. The therapists tried again to get the group members to respond to what I had said, but nobody wanted to.

Finally, Roger said, "Tell me more about your father."

"Why is everyone interested in that?" I asked.

"Maybe it's important."

"I have some antagonism with my father."

Roger waved his hand. "The subconscious doesn't know words like antagonism; the subconscious knows words like love and hate."

I didn't know what to say.

Time was gone, and Roger summed up: "You apparently have some feelings of anger and aggression bubbling up from your subconscious. I want you to chew on it for a while. See if you get anywhere."

Chew on it? I thought; that's all I've been doing, for weeks.

Roger dismissed the group: "Everyone back here at three-thirty sharp this afternoon."

I was much relieved to have the group over. I felt very panicky. My panicky feelings continued as Sarah took me to a sunny room with three tables and some molded plastic chairs.

"How did you like your first group?" asked Sarah.

"I don't know," I answered.

"Did it scare you?"

"Yes, it did."

"You see? Some of those people have problems that are a lot worse than yours."

I didn't answer. There was some small encouragement in the fact that some people were a lot worse off than I was. But not very much. Whatever their problems were, mine were still very real to me, and they were still acute. Furthermore, it terrified me to think that my problems might get worse and become as bad as theirs. For I was now fully aware how my feelings could take a course of their own and run straight out of my control.

Vicky joined us in the small room. Sarah had taken some folders from a filing cabinet in the corner. "These are three different personality profile tests. I want both of you to take them all. This is tedious stuff; there's no use pretending otherwise. But it will give us a place to start."

I sat at the first table, and Vicky sat at the next one, her back to me. "These tests are timed," Sarah continued, "But pay no attention to the time limits. Just finish them as quickly as you can." She left, and I worked on the tests.

The tests were full of personality questions like this one:

In my spare time, I would most prefer to:

(a) read a book
(b) watch television
(c) do a chore
(d) have recreation
(e) sleep

But Sarah was right; the tests were long and tedious. I found myself choosing answers quickly, without much thought.

Just before noon, Vicky began to cry. I looked at her, but I could not see her face. Her arms were folded on the table, and her head was down on her arms. She sobbed and sobbed, her shoulders moving up and down. I felt terrible; I wanted to do something for her. I wanted to go and put an arm around her, but I was too inhibited. I merely sat where I was until, finally, she stopped.

We had lunch in the small cafeteria. There were approximately thirty patients and half a dozen staff. There was little talking. Most of the patients were sullen and uncommunicative. I had no appetite: I ate some gelatin and drank some milk. After lunch, Vicky and I finished the tests. Then we had free time, but I found nothing to do. I went briefly into the game room downstairs where some people were playing pool or cards. I felt it was a miserable place. I went into the corridor, where the windows went from ceiling to floor. For a long time, I stared across the highway, out across the fields, covered with snow. The sky was now overcast, and a few snowflakes were blowing through the air. I felt useless.

At three-thirty, we had group therapy again, in the lounge. This time, our group was combined with another group. The other group had a new person, Elaine, an attractive young farmer's wife. She was thin, but shapely, and she wore a red ribbon in her black hair. She was afraid of choking to death; choking symptoms were apparently seizing her at various times, and she couldn't get any air. She explained this to the group.

"Does anyone want to ask anything?" asked Roger. I could see by now how much the therapists wanted the group members to respond to one another's problems, and how they almost never did.

Roger turned to Gus, in the corner. "Gus, what do you think of what Elaine has told us?"

Gus was leaning back in his chair. He was very fat. His mouth was hanging open, and his eyes were closed.

Gus opened his eyes halfway. "Huh?"

"I said, what do you think of Elaine's problem? Wake up and get with us."

Gus opened his eyes a bit more. "Huh?"

"Wake up!" snapped Sarah. "Wake up and sit up! You're not here to sleep!"

"It's the medication," slurred Gus.

"Sit up! I don't care about your medication, and neither do the rest of these people!"

"It's the medication," he repeated. "It makes me real drowsy."

"You be drowsy on your own time! Now sit up!"

Gus sat up and rubbed his eyes. "I'll try to stay awake."

"That's better," said Roger. "Louise wants to go home this weekend. Just for Saturday and Sunday. What do you people think about that?" He was addressing the entire group.

"Let her go home," said Norman loudly.

"Why?" asked Roger.

"Because anything's better'n this place." A few people laughed.

"How about the rest of you?" asked Sarah. "Do you think Louise should spend a couple of days at home?"

Nobody answered.

"Why do you want to go home, Louise?" asked Roger.

Louise had her legs crossed, and in her lap her hands had her handkerchief pressed into a ball. "I need to go home and be with my husband."

"Why?"

"He wants me to come home, and I want to be with him."

"Does he need you?"

"Oh yes, I'm sure he does."

Then Rachel spoke. She was a young woman who was a therapist with the other group. "Why does he need you?"

"He needs me to do things."

"Such as?"

"Oh, you know, take care of things."

Then Rachel got sarcastic. "He needs you to cook the meals and wash the dishes and scrub the floors?"

"Yes."

"Do the laundry, clean the house, do the ironing?"

"Yes, that too."

"This makes me sick," said Rachel sharply. "He needs you to do all this stuff! What do *you* need?! Who is suffering here? You or him? What about what *you* need?"

"He loves me very much," said Louise, now beginning to cry. "He loves me, and he cares for me."

"I'll bet."

"My husband is a wonderful man."

"Sure he is, just as long as you make his bed, do his laundry, do his ironing, cook his meals, and clean up after him."

"My husband is a wonderful man!" insisted Louise, sobbing.

"Has he ever come here once, to speak to the therapists? Has he ever tried to understand what is going on with you?"

"No, but he brings me here on Monday and picks me up on Friday."

"Oh, how wonderful," said Rachel with great sarcasm.

Roger joined in. "You have some terrible anger for your husband, Louise. Can you understand that?"

She shook her head no, still sobbing.

"Louise, do you recognize any of your feelings?" demanded Roger. He picked up a heavy ashtray of green glass and emptied it into the waste basket. He went to where Louise was sitting and stood in front of her. "Get mad," he demanded. He held out the ashtray. "Get mad, and throw this. Throw it at me, or throw it through the window, I don't care. But get mad."

He continued to hold out the ashtray for some moments, but Louise continued to sob. She did not look up, and she did not accept the ashtray.

I was shocked at the way the therapists were badgering Louise. My heart was beating rapidly and my palms were sweating.

After the group was over, I could not help cornering Sarah in the hall. "What on earth were you people trying to do to that poor woman?"

"Are you an expert on therapy already?" she answered sharply.

"No, but—"

"Is it time for you to tell us how to do our jobs?"

I got angry. "No, but I know something about human beings and decent treatment."

"Do you?" she asked. "What do you know about your own feelings?"

"What's that got to do with it?"

"It's got everything to do with it. There's not a patient here, you included, who knows a thing about his own feelings."

I was mad. "Go to hell," I said tightly.

She smiled. "Good. That's more like it. Now, if you'll excuse me, I'm late for an appointment." And she left.

That was one of my first lessons. As patients, most of us were out of touch with our own feelings. The therapists wanted us to express the feelings we had, even if the feelings were not "acceptable."

That night, at home, I went over all of it with Judy. I explained to her the idea of getting in touch with feelings, of recognizing and acknowledging your real feelings.

"Is that real important?" she asked.

"The therapists seem to think it's important," I answered. "I don't know if it's important for me. I don't know how it's going to help me." Then I didn't talk more, for I was exhausted.

In the days that followed, the mental health unit was the center of my routine. Each morning, I drove to the hospital, filled with fear. Was my life, as I knew it, over? Could I survive? Each night I drove home with feelings of disbelief and disorientation.

I became accustomed to the routines of our therapy group. It became obvious to me how many of the patients were locked into their behavior patterns, which caused them so much trouble. They either could not change, or they had no desire to change. For whatever reason, they were unable to move off of the square they were on. This frightened me, because I began to see the same problem in myself; I seemed to be repeating the same defeating feelings over and over, asking the same questions again and again, making no progress.

DeeAnn was the main therapist in our group; she was the one who was always present. She was simply not effective. I later learned that she had had very little experience at therapy. She seemed uncertain most of the time and exerted very little group leadership. She often seconded what other people said, but she rarely took the lead. She was not capable of providing the leadership I needed.

I was not prepared to be patient; I wanted to find the "answer." I always felt discouraged when I discovered that Sarah would not be with our group on a particular day but that DeeAnn would be.

The staff psychiatrist was no better. He was doing some kind of exchange research, and would soon be returning to his own country. He met with each group just once a week. He seemed distracted and in a hurry. When I spoke to him, he did not look at me, and he fidgeted with his beard. I did not feel any confidence in him, and I don't think others did, either. I did not get to know a great deal about him, as he was with us so rarely.

We spent part of each day in what was called "occupational therapy." It was really arts and crafts. We made little ashtrays out of scraps of ceramic tile and grouting compound. We did decoupage. We painted with oils and water colors. We did some woodworking. Whenever one of us finished a project, DeeAnn would hold it up and say, "Look at this lovely ashtray! Isn't this fine work? Good, Gus, *very* good."

I thought it was patronizing and stupid. There we were, a group of adults, being treated like preschoolers.

We also spent part of each day in "recreational therapy." It was sometimes board games, such as checkers or chess, sometimes shooting pool or playing ping-pong. Sometimes it was volleyball.

One day I was playing Chinese checkers with Norman. It was incredibly boring.

"How long have you been here, Norman?" I asked.

"About three weeks."

"When will you be getting out?"

"I don't know," he said with a large smile.

"Don't you care?"

"Not really. I like it here. I like the games."

I was confused. "I've heard you complain, lots of times."

"I hate the group therapy. Other than that, I like it here. I like the games."

I felt impatient. "You can't spend the rest of your life in places like this."

"Why not?"

"Because there's more to life. There are things to do, things to accomplish."

He smiled again. "You're welcome to your opinion. It's your move, by the way."

I had as many conversations, in private, with Sarah, as I could manage. One day she said to me, "We like to have patients like you. Don't get me wrong; I'm not happy that you're suffering so much that you need to be here."

"Why do you like to have patients like me?"

"Because you have intelligence; you're used to taking leadership. You make our jobs a little easier."

"In group, you mean?"

"Yes. You are a good model. You set a good example for other patients."

For some reason, I was irritated. "That's all well and good, but it's not doing me any good. I'm not getting any better."

"Are you sure?"

"Yes, I'm sure; I'm still terrified, I still can't sleep. I'm still disoriented, and I still don't know why. I still don't have an answer."

"Don't be so compulsive about the answer."

"That's easy for you to say."

One afternoon, at the beginning of recreational therapy, Sarah wanted the group to go bowling.

"Why?" asked Norman.

"Let's do something different. Let's get away from here and do something different."

Most of the patients were unenthused. They did not get very excited about changes in their routine. Gus was heavily medicated again, and he said, "I vote we stay here."

"Who said anything about a vote?" asked Sarah.

"Let's be democratic," slurred Gus. "I vote to stay here."

Jessica and Jeanette sat in the corner, sullen and quiet. Louise picked at her handkerchief and did not speak.

Then Sarah looked at me. She did not speak, but I knew what she wanted. I was still suffering bitterly, and I did not feel that my experience here, as a mental patient, was helping me very much. More than anything else, I wanted help. Yet, I had been a leadership person for a number of years, and I was accustomed to getting things done. So I stood up.

"Let's go bowling," I said.

"What for?" said Gus.

"Just to do something different. Let's get off our rear ends and do something."

It was enough. The group voted to go bowling. When we got there, we occupied several lanes. There were other people at the bowling lanes who identified us as a group of "crazies." They smirked at us and stared. They were obviously making jokes about us, and often burst into laughter. It was the first time in my life I had ever experienced that kind of humiliation.

One afternoon, after being at the hospital for several days, I was having a long talk with Sarah. On other occasions, we had talked about my childhood, my father, my mother, my brothers and sisters, and my friends. She had asked me about my childhood feelings and what kinds of activities I had participated in. I liked Sarah very much and respected her. She was attractive, warm, and intelligent.

On this particular afternoon, she was talking with me about my test results.

"Your tests show that you are intelligent, alert to the world around you, and that you have almost no self-esteem."

I shrugged. None of this was new to me.

"You don't like yourself very much at all," she continued. "I guess you knew that already, though."

"Yes, I know it."

"What do you do with it?"

I felt very discouraged. "Sarah, I've got to find the answer. I want to know what's happening to trigger all of this panic and terror. I've *got* to know."

"You're compulsive."

"I've got to know."

"Listen to me," she said. "This is not the movies. In the movies, some psychiatrist who looks like Freud digs and digs into the poor slob's life until he finds that traumatic moment, buried in the subconscious for years and years. Then everything is solved. The suffering goes away, and the poor slob walks off into the sunset. This is not the movies. This is real."

"You mean there might not be any cause for my feelings?"

"Oh yes, there's a cause, but maybe not the kind of cause you want to find. You want one thing or one event.

Your suffering could be a culmination of a whole lot of things."

Discouraged, I asked her a question I was terrified to ask: "Am I having a nervous breakdown?"

"You can call it that if you want, but we don't like to use that term."

"Why not?"

"It's too vague; it doesn't mean anything."

"But that's what I'm having."

"I said if you want to, you can call it that. If it makes you feel any better, O.K., you're having a nervous breakdown. You're having a mental breakdown."

I looked down and felt the tears stinging my eyes. There it was, the name that terrified me: *breakdown*. A mental breakdown. A nervous breakdown. And it was happening to me. To *me*, not somebody else.

Sarah sensed my fear and consoled me as best she could. "A breakdown is so vague that it doesn't mean anything. It's like saying a car broke down. It can mean anything: the car ran out of gas, the battery went dead, almost anything."

"Can I get over it? Can I get well?"

"You can get well," she said. "Your anxiety is very acute. I can't remember a patient with anxiety this acute for this length of time. In most of the patients I've known, acute anxiety has a short life; it comes and goes rather quickly. The rest of the time, their anxiety is at a lower level."

"But what's causing me to be this way?" I asked.

"There you go again. Let me tell you what I can tell you. Many times people with generalized anxiety come from families with extremely high expectations. It doesn't surprise me that you grew up in a clergy family. I've seen this before; ministers' children or rabbis' children usually hold themselves up against the highest measuring stick. Perfection, almost. A person who expects to be perfect is always a failure."

"Is this my problem?"

"It could very well be a big part of it. Can you succeed?"

"At what?"

"At anything. Do you ever acknowledge that you have succeeded at anything?"

"I don't know."

"I'll bet you don't. Can you take credit for doing something really well, or do you say, 'Oh, it's really nothing'? Or do you say, 'Well, I could have done it even better'?"

I felt discovered. I nodded my head yes.

"Then I'm right. You can't succeed. Are you a good teacher?"

Embarrassed, I nodded my head.

"Say it."

"I'm a good teacher," I said, still embarrassed.

"Do you believe it?"

"I don't know."

"It's wrong to appreciate yourself, isn't that so?"

"I'm not sure what's so."

"You don't believe it, do you?"

"I don't know!" I felt helpless.

"Do you see why I tell you to know yourself?" she asked. "You need to know yourself and appreciate yourself. I can't give you the whole answer, but I think you'd better start there: figure out who you really are."

I wasn't sure how she was right, but I felt she was saying something important.

The longer I stayed at the mental hospital, the more accustomed I became to bizarre behavior. One afternoon during free time, I was walking down the hallway toward the game room.

I heard a small voice: "Hey."

I stopped and turned. It was Diane. She was standing at the entrance to her room, and she was naked.

I was startled. She smiled and said, "Wanna come in?" For a moment, I stood there dumbly, staring at her thin body. Then I felt very embarrassed, turned, and headed on down the hallway. I walked rapidly and did not look back.

I went on downstairs and wondered if I should tell Sarah and DeeAnn about this. I didn't want to be a "tattle-tale," but I knew the staff were concerned about Diane and considered her to be potentially suicidal.

The wisest thing, I decided, would be to tell them about Diane and then let them decide what to do, if anything. I went to the office, where both women were sitting and doing paperwork.

"What is it, Jim?"

"I just saw Diane. She was standing at her doorway naked, and she invited me into her room."

DeeAnn put her papers down and stood up. "I'll go and take care of it," she said quietly.

"I'm not telling you this to get her into any trouble," I said quickly.

"We know that," said Sarah. "You're just concerned about her."

The next morning at group, Sarah, DeeAnn, and Roger, all confronted Diane with the event.

"Tell us what you did, Diane," said Roger.

Diane smiled and looked down. She was red. She mumbled something.

"Speak up!" snapped Sarah.

"I just took my clothes off," she said quietly.

"No, you didn't just take your clothes off," said Sarah. "What else did you do?"

Diane had a silly smile. "I showed myself to him and to

him." She pointed to Norman and to me. I felt embarrassed and looked down. Norman smiled and covered his face to keep from laughing.

What on earth am I doing here?, I asked myself for perhaps the hundredth time.

Roger went on: "Diane, why did you exhibit yourself?"

"I don't know."

"Speak up."

"I don't know."

"Look up," said Sarah sharply. "Look up and pay attention. Why did you exhibit yourself?"

Diane would not answer. She shook her head firmly and said loudly, "I don't know."

"Of course you know," said Sarah. "You wanted attention. Right?"

"I'm not sure."

"Dammit, of course you're sure. You wanted attention. If you take your clothes off and exhibit yourself, you want attention. That's simple enough, isn't it?"

"O.K., I wanted attention."

"Speak up."

"I wanted attention!"

"That's better," said Roger. "Diane, when will you understand that you'll never get better until you stop lying? Isn't that plain to you yet?"

"I don't know."

"When you begin to acknowledge some of your feelings, and then state them honestly, you may begin to get better."

This event gave me a jolt, because I recognized that what Roger was saying applied to me just as certainly as it applied to Diane. That night I had searched for the dog in the blizzard, was that any less bizarre than Diane's taking her clothes off? True, I had gone into the woods alone, while

Diane had exhibited herself publicly, but was that really a difference? How sick was I?

After several more days passed, I moved toward the conclusion that the mental hospital was not really for me. Except for those conversations with Sarah, which were rare, my experience was not good.

In group therapy, we were usually spinning our wheels in the same ruts. Louise stayed depressed. Norman continued to be without motivation. Jessica and Jeanette remained sullen and uncooperative. I felt I got very little personal attention, and very little help; we spent too much time trying to urge other patients to cooperate in their own recovery.

The mental health center seemed to have the same problems that most public agencies have: it was trying to meet many different human needs on limited resources.

There was only one psychiatrist. The other therapists had minimum training and minimum experience. The staff members did not neglect their responsibilities, but neither did they seem to have much enthusiasm for their work. Mostly, they just seemed tired.

While I was there, I felt a great humiliation. It appalled me that here I was, helpless and confused, in a mental institution with all these crazy people. How could it be happening to me?

On the positive side, I did feel some relief in the knowledge that I was doing something to try to figure out my problem. At least I was trying.

A few days longer, and I felt I saw even more limitations of the hospital and its routines. In addition to the scarcity of personal attention, there seemed to be a general listlessness. Many of the patients were so heavily medicated that they were nearly comatose. They sat in group therapy scarcely awake, their eyelids heavy. They were often unable to respond to questions.

Even though some of each day was structured, much of it was not. I remember a lot of patients sitting or standing around during free time and just sulking with each other.

As unstable as I felt, it was hard for me to make any decision. But I decided that the hospital was not for me. I told Sarah of this decision.

"Aren't we helping you?" she asked.

"A little," I admitted. "But not enough to satisfy me. I want more. I want more progress."

"There are a lot of patients here," she said. "We can't give each one what we'd like to give."

"I know," I said. "I'm not criticizing. I just don't think this is the best thing for me."

"What is, then?"

"I don't know," I said. "I wish I did."

"Have you decided for sure, then?" she asked.

"Yes."

"That's good. You have a good brain. You have to use it and trust it."

We shook hands. I looked into her eyes. She smiled at me. "Go get 'em in the real world," she said, laughing.

Sarah was not a person I would quickly forget. I went back to my regular world and started the second semester on time.

Four

My feelings of terror and panic stayed with me every day and every night. I still could not eat or sleep, day after day, and night after night. Each morning I wondered if I could make it through the day. I still didn't know what was causing the problem.

In desperation, I began to pray. Each morning before I went to school, I walked across the snow and ice into the fields behind our house. I stood in the cold, watching the sun rise. I pleaded with God: "Help me," I sobbed. "Help me. Heal me. Please, God, heal me."

I had a book of meditations by John Baillie that Dick Dutton had given me. Each morning after I got to the school parking lot, I sat in my car and read that day's meditation.

Days of despair turned into weeks of despair.

I would sit at school in informal coffee groups. Others talked and laughed and swapped stories while I was weeping inwardly with despair. It was terribly discouraging. I wanted to be part of them. I wanted to be having fun, too.

When I taught classes, I had to force my mind to focus on the material at hand. At times my mind tore off on its own, inventing fearful and hideous consequences for my life; at those times I had to force my mind to refocus on the material we were discussing and the questions the students were asking. I thought this was pitiful and wondered how long I could keep it up.

I threw myself into my work. I kept as busy as possible. I created as much busy work as I could: I had the students keep a notebook current, in which they wrote daily essays of one paragraph. I graded all the paragraphs and wrote directions for improvement. I bought a snap-down folder for each student and collected his or her paragraphs in order. I made it plain to the students that this work was strictly for their own personal improvement; it was not work that would affect their grade. What it really was, was busywork to keep me absorbed.

I told the college president of my problem. I'm not sure why I did, for while he was a nice man, I had never had a close relationship with him. Maybe I wanted sympathy. In any case, he was very supportive. He told me that if I ever needed time off, he would stand behind me. That gave me a feeling of relief.

I constantly hashed it over with Judy. One morning as we were talking, she reminded me, "I think we're going over the same ground again and again."

"I know we are," I admitted.

"Do you think maybe you gave up on the therapy too soon?"

"I don't know," I said. "It's possible."

"You could just go one night a week, to one of those adult groups; didn't Sarah suggest that?"

She had. "But it seems like the therapy was just the same repetition; you, know, spinning your wheels over and over in the same place."

"Like we do at home," said Judy.

"Yes, and I'll tell you something else," I said. "A lot of those people in therapy act like they don't care if they change or not. It's like they've resigned themselves to being the way they are—they *don't care* if they change or not!"

"But you do."

"Absolutely. No matter what, I'm not going to give in to this thing. I will never accept that this is the way I have to be!"

And that was true. Whatever else I didn't have, I had perseverance.

The next day turned out to be a traumatic one. Just before supper, Judy and I were standing in the L portion of our living room, which was our dining area. We looked into the kitchen where Jason was standing, holding one of his toy trucks.

Above him on the counter, stew was cooking in the electric skillet; steam poured out around the edge of the skillet lid. The electric cord that was attached to the skillet had formed a loop which extended over and below the edge of the counter. Jason reached up and pulled on the cord.

I could see it happening, but I was paralyzed for an instant and couldn't move. The electric skillet tumbled on top of him, turning over as it fell. The skillet slammed against his head and knocked him to the floor. Boiling grease and gravy covered his neck, shoulders, and torso. Jason lay on the floor, screaming at the top of his lungs.

Filled with panic, I ran into the kitchen. The grease and gravy had made the floor very slick and I fell flat onto the floor, covering myself with the scalding grease.

Jason was screeching and Judy was white with panic. I lay in the hot grease knowing that I had to move, and that I had to get Jason to the hospital quickly. I grabbed him up and slipped again, slamming myself against the counter while I was holding him in my arms.

Judy grabbed a blanket, and we made a mad dash for the car. She sopped up the grease that was on Jason and me as we sped for town. Jason cried and cried. I was nearly hysterical with fear and anger. I sped through stop signs and stop lights, honking my horn and driving much too fast.

When we got to the hospital emergency room, there was an examination room available immediately, and the attending physician took it in stride. "Just be calm," he said to me.

I sat down on a chair in the corner. My heart was racing, and I felt my pulse beating in my head. I was dizzy. The doctor and the nurse cut away Jason's clothes and began to clean him up. He was still crying, and Judy was standing nearby with the tears shining in her eyes.

Jason had third degree burns on the right part of his neck, his right shoulder and upper arm, and on the right side of his chest and stomach. The nurse applied an ointment to his burns, and then covered all of the burned area with a gauze bandage, wrapped around him like a shoulder harness.

Eventually, he calmed down and the doctor spoke to us.

"How are you?" he asked me.

"I'm O.K."

"Are you burned?"

"I don't think so," I said. "It's just my clothes."

"O.K." He gave us a tube of ointment. "Do you have gauze bandages at home?"

Judy said we did.

"You'll need to change this dressing every day, and put on new ointment. Put a tight-fitting shirt on him; it'll hold the dressing in place, and he'll be less likely to pull it loose."

"Will he be O.K.?" I asked.

"I think so. Keep changing the dressing each day and then bring him back in next week. I'd like to look at him."

When we left, I had to pause for a moment and lean against the doorway; I felt shaky and dizzy. On the way home, Judy said, "We don't have any supper at home."

I thought of the kitchen at home, the electric skillet lying in the middle of the floor, and the grease slopped all over. The image made me very sad, and I felt the tears stinging my eyes.

"We'll get a hamburger on the way home," I said. Jason was on Judy's lap; he was no longer crying, but the tears had dried on his face in dirty smudges.

When we got home, I cleaned up the kitchen and Judy went upstairs to put Jason to bed. It took more than an hour to get him completely calmed down and comfortable, until he was sleeping soundly.

When Judy came downstairs I said, "I'm going to take your advice," I said suddenly. "I'm going to sign up for one of those therapy groups at night."

"What changed your mind?"

"You saw how I reacted tonight. I'm terrified by everything that happens. I can't take anything in stride."

"Jim, what happened tonight was very scary! I was terrified! Anyone would have been."

"I know," I said. "But you'll get over it. I won't. It'll shake me up for days." I felt wretched and incompetent. "I've gone from being terrified of nothing, to being terrified of nothing and everything."

"I think the group therapy is a good idea," she said. She put her hand on my arm. "But everyone I know would have been terrified by what happened to Jason tonight." Throughout my long ordeal, Judy was to keep up this kind of realism and support.

But I wanted her to see my point. "I'm scared of everything," I said. "I'm scared of classes; I'm scared of going to bed; I'm scared of having free time. The whole world is terrifying to me. Even if this had never happened tonight, the facts would still be the facts."

We held each other for awhile. "I guess you'd better go then," she said.

"I have to try something," I said. "I've got to do something."

I called Sarah the next day, and she got me enrolled in one of the evening therapy groups. The group met at the mental health center on Thursday nights. So, beginning in late February, I renewed my relationship with that unit, one night a week.

The group met in the game room. We sat on the plastic chairs, arranged in a circle. I met the therapist, whose name was Gerald, and then I was introduced to the ten people who made up the group. All of them were strangers to me.

The first night I was there, all our time was taken by the problems of a particularly miserable woman. Her name was Gayle. She was in her thirties, and very, very fat. It looked as though she seldom washed. Her hair was stringy and clumped together; her dress was dirty and shapeless. Her fingernails were chewed all the way down and her hands were coated with grime.

She told us her ex-husband was a drunk who was trying to kill her. He had been ordered by a judge not to come into the village where she lived, but he had been threatening her anyway. In addition, he had a criminal record of assault and battery.

Gayle was very frightened. She cried continually as she tried to speak, and she clutched a soiled handkerchief in her hands.

"Is there anyone to help you?" asked Gerald. "Is there anyone with you who can give you any help?"

"I used to count on Jamie, but he's got himself in a bad crowd, and now he's getting into his own trouble."

"Gayle, tell us who Jamie is."

"He's my stepson. He lives with me."

"How old is Jamie?"

"He's seventeen. He's got himself in a bad crowd. He was in jail last week for drunk driving. I used to count on him to help me, but he's too far into this bad crowd."

"Do you have a car, Gayle?"

"We used to have Jamie's car, but they took his license away."

"How do you run errands, then? How do you get to the grocery store?"

"I don't know how we'll do it; we used to use Jamie's car." Then she broke down and cried loudly. She couldn't speak anymore.

The rest of us were silent for several moments while she composed herself. Then Gerald began to ask her a few more questions.

"Besides Jamie, how many children do you have living with you?"

"Five."

"Do you have any income besides public aid?"

She shook her head.

"Have you told us everything? Is there anything else you want to tell us?"

She fought to control herself and said: "They want to take my youngest child away."

"Who is 'they'?"

"Department of Family Services. They want to take my two-year-old away and put him in a foster home. They say my home's not fit."

"The two-year-old. What's his name?"

"Joe. They want to take him away! They say my home's not fit!" Then she broke down again and wept bitterly.

For a few moments, the rest of us were quiet. I felt deeply moved and shaken. How terrifying life could become! How miserable were some people's lives, and how great their suffering was. I felt ashamed that I, with almost no problems that I could see, should be unable to live effectively.

Then Gerald asked the group: "Does anyone have anything to say to Gayle?"

A thin woman, named Kate, who chain-smoked Camel cigarettes, spoke up: "I think they should throw the slob in jail."

"You mean the husband?" someone asked.

"I mean the *ex*-husband," Kate corrected. Kate had a sharp tongue and was very opinionated. She sat continually with her legs crossed, wagging the foot that was off the floor, and resting her elbow on her knee. "They ought to lock him up and throw away the key. People like that have no right to be running around free. But then, what can you expect from a man?"

Kate's attack on men slowed down the conversation, and then a man named Richie spoke. He was neatly dressed and seemed intelligent. "Let's suppose the law has done all that it's going to do. If that's the case, what advice can we give her?" He shrugged. "I don't know, to tell you the truth."

Gerald said, "Gayle, there is counseling for children at the center here. Have you ever thought of bringing Joe for counseling?"

"He's only two."

"There is therapy for children that young. People are trained for it."

Apparently the thought of her two-year-old needing therapy, at such a young age, caused Gayle to cry again.

After many more questions, it was determined that Gayle had no friends or relatives who could be with her, to help her. Finally, Gerald told her, "I'll talk with Department of Family Services. They can help you out with your transportation problem. In addition, I want you to call me every day, here, and report to me how things are going. Is that a deal?"

She nodded her head up and down, still sobbing and unable to speak.

After the group was over, I talked with Richie for a while in the lobby. We were the same age, and we were both teachers. I found it easy to talk with him. He was having a problem similar to mine, except that he was going through a divorce and a court fight for custody of the children.

I told him how ashamed I felt of my own problem, after hearing of Gayle's terrible suffering and real threats.

"Oh you can't feel that way," he said. "We all have to come from where we're at. It's no use comparing yourself to the other people."

I nodded in agreement.

"There's always somebody worse off than you are," he said. "It's even true of Gayle. Somewhere, somebody is worse off than she is."

"Do you ever get much personal attention in this group?" I asked.

"Not much. But I think there's some value in helping other people. It develops your skill at seeing problems, what causes them, and what helps to solve them. It gives you greater problem-solving ability."

I was disappointed, because I wanted help with my problem. But I decided to think about what he was saying.

On my second night at the group, Gerald asked me to explain my problem to the group, which I did. I had spoken of it so many times, I was able to summarize briefly and clearly.

"So what are you afraid of?" asked Kate.

"That's just it," I said. "I don't know. I have all the symptoms of fear, but no cause."

"There has to be something," she said.

"I know that," I said, irritated. "But whatever it is, I can't identify it."

"It doesn't make any sense," she said glibly.

Now I was furious and ashamed; she was making my problem seem so trivial. "Of course it doesn't make any sense!" I snapped. "If it made any sense, I wouldn't be here!"

Then Gerald stepped in: "Kate, if all our problems were subject to logic, we wouldn't need mental health services. If your problems were the kind that could be solved by your own logic, you wouldn't need to be here tonight."

Kate looked down. She was an alcoholic.

Other members of the group tried to make what contributions they could, but my condition was not familiar to them. It was different from what they were used to.

On another night, Richie spoke to the group about his divorce and his custody crisis. His wife had left him, but she wanted to take the two children with her. A judge had conducted a hearing but had not yet reached a decision. At present, the two children were living with Richie.

"What are your chances?" asked Kate.

"I don't know. Judges almost always side with the woman in a custody case. The man doesn't usually have a chance."

"But she's the one who left the marriage, not you!" insisted Kate.

"I know that, and you know it, but it might not cut it with the judge."

Gerald asked him, "Do you still love your wife?"

Richie looked down for a moment. "I suppose so. I can't really say. I'm too mad at her for doing this. Look, if she wants to leave, I suppose that's her right. But she has no right to take the children."

"She left; she gave up her rights," seconded Kate.

"That's how I feel. Every night, I go into the children's bedroom and watch them sleeping. I wonder if this is the last day they'll be with me." Richie wanted to go on, but his eyes were glistening with tears, and he shook his head. "Go ahead. Talk to somebody else for a while."

My heart froze in terror as I listened to him. I was very afraid that I would drive Judy beyond the limits of her patience and she would leave, taking Jason with her. The thought paralyzed me.

Another night, most of the session was taken up with Ralph, an alcoholic. He had had a couple of homosexual experiences earlier in his adult life. He and his wife were trying to raise a family of three small children on very little income. He was afraid of losing his job—in the past, his drinking had caused him to lose several jobs. He was trying desperately to get through each day.

"Are you a homosexual?" asked Gerald.

Ralph shook his head slowly from side to side. "I don't think so, no."

"Do you want to be a homosexual?"

"No. Absolutely not."

"Why not?"

Ralph looked down. He was a large man with thick brown hair. He wore glasses. "I know what I want in life. I want my wife and children, I want us to have a good life together. I want a good job that is steady."

"You have all that now, don't you?" asked Richie.

"Yes," he nodded.

"Then you have what you want, and you know how to keep it. You should have it made."

Ralph shook his head slowly. "I'm weak . . . I'm too weak. I've had it made in the past, and then I started drinking. Or something else. I'm just weak." He bit his lip and quit talking.

As I heard these tragic, desperate stories, I was afraid my own problems would get much worse. I was swollen with panic. Because of my intense emotional pain and anxiety, I, like the others, was unable to get outside myself for long.

I could see again the limited benefits of the group experience. Everyone wanted attention, and everyone got very little personal attention. Gerald, the leader, was kind and sensitive, and he tried hard not to dominate the group. He asked occasional questions. He wanted the members of the group to help each other, and for the most part, they were alert and helpful to one another's needs. But most of us were not satisfied with this approach. We wanted Gerald to give each of us an answer. I was no different. I wanted my problem solved; I wanted an answer. I was sorry that others were hurting, but *I wanted my problem solved*. That was why I was there.

I did understand the value of group problem-solving, and therefore I was not tempted to leave the group. I stayed with it for quite a long time. I had the feeling once again that at least I was doing something. Fighting back.

The longer I stayed with the group, the more I looked at myself and at my past. I was following Sarah's advice: I was getting to know myself.

There were now two things that seemed important to me, if I hoped to fight back. The first was, get in touch with my feelings. I had to learn to identify my *real* feelings and acknowledge them clearly. The second, which would hopefully follow the first, was to get in touch with myself. I needed to know myself.

There was progress. As the weeks passed, I learned a lot about myself, who I was and what kind of person I was.

One discovery I had made was that I didn't like myself. I was a person without self-respect. I had almost no sense of my own worth. Yet, by almost any objective standard, I was very successful.

I wished I had made a more unique discovery. For what do we hear more often than, "I don't have any self-respect," or, "I guess I don't like myself very much"? What my current experience was telling me, though, was that as common as this was, disliking myself over a period of time might now be causing me serious emotional problems. If you dislike yourself long enough, under the right conditions, it can be dangerous.

As I looked back over my life, I could see a clear pattern: I had almost always been motivated by a strong need to please others. I had been raised in a Protestant parsonage. As a "preacher's kid," I felt different and separate from others. My need for approval was powerful, and it affected my behavior. Even as a young child I had liked to hide the girls' purses and throw firecrackers into the school restrooms. I thought if I could have some reputation as a clown, I would be perceived as just as "secular" as anyone else.

As an adolescent, I had nearly always succumbed to peer pressure. I did nearly everything like everyone else because that was the way to be liked. Anything I did—the clothes I wore, the girls I dated, the teams I tried out for—I did to please someone else. I am convinced I behaved that way to get the approval of others, since I did not have my own approval. There's nothing unusual about this—it's just that I was beginning to see it as a clear pattern in my own life.

In late adolescence and early adulthood, it was more of the same. The peer groups looked a little different, but I tried just as hard to please them. In the fraternity I joined, I tried to chug beer to get approval and laughs. I tried to whip myself into a frenzy over a rope pull (tug of war) against another fraternity. It didn't work. I never really cared if we won or not. When we lost, though, I put on a good act of grief and sadness. Anything to please others.

Some of the time in college, instead of going to classes, I would smoke cigarettes and play cards in the grill section of the student union. I did not like playing cards, drinking beer, or pulling ropes. But I hoped I was impressing somebody.

I hardly ever had an opinion about anything (girls and athletics excepted), but when I did, if someone expressed the opposite view, I usually discarded my own in a hurry.

In order to impress girls, I would lie, deceive, pretend,

twist myself into almost any shape. I always wanted to date the most beautiful and popular girls in school in order that I might make a big impression on whoever might be watching. I worked hard at that.

In the sixties, I was very active in the anti-war protest movement. I feel now, as I reflect, that many of my adult opinions—especially those of an anti-establishment nature—were also devices to please others. Most of the people who were my friends and associates were part of the anti-war movement. Those were the people I wanted to impress. I wanted to feel superior to "squares" and other people who were part of the establishment. I might add that I believed then, and still do, that wars should be stopped, along with the other forms of violence we commit against ourselves and our world. I am proud of the fact that I had beliefs and that I stood up for those beliefs. But all the while, I was also using my public proclamations to meet my own need: I was using this sphere of my life to get approval.

This was the *me* that I was discovering, through my weekly trips to group therapy, my conversations with Judy and a few intimate friends, my reading, and my thinking.

I had been bent out of shape for years.

It was very discouraging; was it likely that others would respect me if I had no respect for myself? I felt ashamed as this self-portrait became clearer to me, and I felt a deep sense of regret: all those years I had worked so hard to keep the real me from surfacing.

There was a second message that I was getting during this period. That message seemed to be a corollary of the first: Be me. Be *honest*. All the soundest advice I could ferret out seemed to be saying, "Part of your problem is this essential dishonesty. Part of your anguish may be a consequence of years of lying. Quit lying. Express yourself."

Being me was just about as hard as anything I ever

tried. But I was suffering badly and I wanted to get well. So I tried being me. A little at a time, I tried to be myself. I wasn't very good at it, but how could I be? I had thirty years of lying to overcome.

I practiced on Judy, who was my constant support throughout the whole trying experience. In my talks with her, I tried to speak the truth, to express my real feelings honestly, and to do so in a simple, straightforward manner. It was very, very difficult.

I began to try the same thing with my closest friends. If a friend invited me to do something I didn't want to do, I tried saying, "No, thank you." If a friend stated an opinion I did not share, I tried saying, "I disagree."

My first attempts were often pretty clumsy. I would blurt out, "You are wrong!" or, "You make me angry." Luckily, I had some friendships that were strong enough to suffer along with me.

Learning to disagree with people, learning to risk their possible disapproval—this was a hard and threatening experience. But I was learning, and I am witness to the fact that it can be learned. I am also witness to the fact that if we do not learn this ability, the consequences may turn out to be serious, and even dangerous.

I began to force myself to disagree out loud with people, learning to risk their possible disapproval. It was difficult. Emotionally, it seemed to me to be too risky. "If I disagree with this person, it might create a conflict." "This guy might get uptight with me and walk away or something." "This guy might not like me if I tell him I don't agree."

One of my earliest attempts to confront a person honestly turned out to be a minor calamity. I had a student named Betsy, who was a very bright girl, but who had very little personal discipline. She frequently failed to do assignments or handed them in late. I had encouraged this over a period of time by accepting her numerous excuses, rather than holding her to the same policies and guidelines other students were expected to meet. I had done this, no doubt, to avoid her disapproval or to avoid a confrontation and to protect my reputation as a "liberal" faculty member.

But on one particular morning, I was determined to confront her and demand that she conform to classroom policies like everybody else. I saw her coming across the large lobby, toward my office. She was dressed as usual, in blue jeans, a flannel shirt, and khaki army coat that reached nearly to her ankles. She wore glasses with wire frames, and her long black hair was utterly straight.

"I thought I'd better come and tell you why I'm late on this paper," she said brightly.

I was tense, not knowing where to begin. "I might as well tell you, Betsy, that I'm very angry with you."

She blinked. "What on earth for?"

"For coming up here with these excuses for late work. I'm tired of listening to your excuses."

"I've always told you what the problem was."

"True, and I've always listened to what you told me. No more. From now on, I expect you to turn your work in on time. I'm going to dock you one letter grade for each day you're late."

She turned sullen. "I don't know what's the matter with you."

"What's the matter with me is listening to too many of your excuses. That's my mistake. But I don't intend to repeat it; it's no good for you or me."

"I can't understand what's going on."

"I can't say it any more clearly."

"What about last Wednesday's assignment?"

"You have until tomorrow. If I don't have it then, you go down one letter grade."

"I don't think I can do it!"

"That's your problem." I was beginning to feel cornered. I hadn't expected her to stand up to me. I had expected her to hear and obey.

"You're not being fair to me," she said.

"I'm sorry you don't think it's fair. But I do, and that's that. Now I suggest you go to the library and get the paper done." I went to my desk, and she walked away angrily, in a hurry.

I sat at my desk and brooded over the confrontation for some time. I had been honest with her, but I didn't have the skill to be honest in a nonthreatening way.

I was clumsy with honesty, like a baby learning to walk. My words didn't often come out the way I hoped they would. And then, of course, there was the problem of balance; perspective. It wasn't just honesty that I had to learn about, it was also selectivity. When was it important to speak my real feelings, and when was it not? We can't be one hundred percent honest, one hundred percent of the time. But it's important for us to know when we are simply saving our energy, as opposed to when we are leaving out some of the truth for fear of disapproval.

I had a lot to learn.

At about this same time, I faced a situation that challenged the spine of my honesty even more. In a nearby farmhouse, lived a farmer whose name was Red; I had never talked with him but had seen him often enough. He appeared to be surly and unfriendly. On a few occasions I had said "hello" to him, but he either made no answer or simply grunted. I had never seen him smile.

He owned two large dogs, partly boxer, that were a nuisance. The dogs often barked through the night, and they tipped over our garbage cans. But more importantly, they ran at, and frightened, our friends who came to visit us. Most of our friends had small children, and their children were usually terrified of the large dogs. Several of our friends had told us they were reluctant to come visit us, because the dogs scared them.

On a couple of occasions, Judy had asked the farmer's wife if there might be some way to control the dogs. Both times, the answer had been, "It's just up to my husband."

"She's scared to death of Red," Judy observed. "She would never disagree with him about anything."

Everyone was afraid of Red, including me. He appeared to be hostile and brutal. But I knew I was going to have to confront him and ask him to control his dogs. The thought terrified me; I was in the midst of my harshest anxieties and did not feel capable of dealing with difficult situations. For several days, I was afraid of the confrontation I knew would have to come. I tried to talk myself out of it; I told myself these were only dogs, that they had never really bitten anyone, and that maybe I should just ignore the whole situation. I told myself that maybe the problem would just disappear.

Every problem seemed so enormous to me; each difficulty that life presented to me seemed so very threatening. But I knew the problem of the dogs would not just disappear, and I knew I would have to find the courage to stand up for my rights and my family's rights.

The day I decided to force the issue, I was shaky throughout the day. At school, my mouth was dry and I was sweating a great deal.

When I drove home from school, I went upstairs, changed my clothes, and put on my boots. I went outside and crossed the field toward Red's barn. I heard his tractor as I neared the barn. I walked around to the barnyard. The scene in front of me was a grim one.

Red was driving his tractor wildly around the barnyard, trying to frighten his own cows. It was the end of February and there had been a thaw; the barnyard was very muddy. Red was driving straight at the cows until they stumbled madly to get out of the way. He headed them into a corner and then laughed when they crashed clumsily against the wooden fence.

My heart pounded as I watched this madness; on his face was a fixed humorless grin, as he terrified one cow after another. At times the cows got their feet stuck in the muck, and they fell. I saw him now as a dangerous and driven man, and I feared for the safety of my family.

Shaken, I went back and told Judy about the incident.

She shook her head in disbelief. "My God, a person like that is dangerous; he could be homicidal."

My stomach was constricted into a ball of fear, but I said, "I'm going back to speak to him; I don't care what he is."

"Oh don't. Please don't. He could be dangerous. I know he has guns."

"I don't want to, but I have to. I can't live my life in terror! I can't be afraid of everything that comes along!"

"But Jim, this is a legitimate fear! You can see that, can't you? It would be insane *not* to be afraid of a person like this!"

"Yes, I do see. But I have to stand up for myself."

"Maybe we could call the police."

"For what? It's not against the law to chase your cows around."

"No, but surely there's some law against letting your dogs run loose and be a nuisance."

I was all tangled up inside. I could see the point of her arguments, but I was also sick and tired of my own terror. "Have you thought of this?" I asked. "Have you thought of what this guy might do to you if you called the sheriff on him? Would that make you feel secure?"

Then Judy got very scared. "What can we do?" she asked. "Janet and David said they won't come and visit any more if those dogs are out. Their children are terrified of those dogs."

That did it. I put my coat back on. "I'm going over there right now. If he wants to kill me, let him; but he's going to know where I stand."

I headed rapidly across the slush in the field, toward the barn again. I was shaking with fear, but I had made a decision and I wasn't going to change it. As I walked, I noticed that the dogs were not in sight, and they had not been in sight earlier, when I had come to the barnyard. *That's odd*, I thought.

When I got to the barn, he was hooking up the milkers. He was at one of the stalls, approximately ten feet from where I stood. "Your name is Red, isn't it?" I said loudly.

He straightened up to look at me. It was the first time I had looked at his face, which was a hard face. His features were gaunt and his eyes were flat. He needed a shave. He wore a red hunting cap and a red plaid jacket. "Yeah. Why?"

"Where are your dogs?" I asked.

"What's it to you?" he blurted.

I wondered if we were going to have a fight. I felt liquid in my knees. "I just want to know," I said.

He spit out some tobacco. "The dogs are dead."

I was shocked. Dead? How could they be dead? I wasn't expecting this information, and it threw me. Finally I said, "Dead? How did that happen?"

He was still looking at me. "It happened because I shot 'em, that's how it happened." He straightened his cap. "Anything else you want?"

I was still shocked and couldn't think of anything to say. The dogs were gone, and so that was solved; but I was supposed to be asserting myself, standing up to him. I had to think for a moment. "I guess not," I finally mumbled.

"Good," he said and went back to work.

Slowly, I made my way back across the field. I felt confused. It wasn't until much later that I felt any relief.

When I got home, I told Judy about it.

"The man is sick," she said. "He should be locked up. I'm terrified."

I could only agree. "I know," I said.

The next day I walked across the fields into the timber. I found Red's footprints soon enough, and in a few moments I found the dogs. They were lying dead, the ropes still around their necks and still tied to a tree. Their legs were stiff with rigor mortis. Their heads were smashed from the bullets. It must have been a hunting rifle, I thought, a powerful gun.

I looked at the pitiful dogs, and I couldn't imagine what had drawn me here. Maybe I wanted to suffer more; to scratch at an open sore. In any case, I felt very sad.

Although the ground was muddy at the surface, it was too hard to dig, so I simply dragged the dogs into a nearby depression and covered their bodies with leaves and snow. Then I started to cry. I felt so sad about the dogs, and I wondered where my life was headed. What could I handle and what could I not handle? There would be other difficulties in my life, there would be other ripples on the water. Could I learn to handle them? Could I gain enough control over my own feelings to face a problem?

As time passed, I began to make some progress toward being honest gracefully. With lots of practice, I got to the point where I could say, "I'm afraid I have to disagree with you," and say it kindly. The other person knew where I stood, but he didn't feel personally threatened. Or, if I didn't like the direction a conversation was taking, I learned to say, "This conversation is making me uncomfortable; could we change the subject?"

Not that it ever gets easy. I suppose being myself will

never be easy, as long as there's the risk of disapproval. But I found that I was willing to take the risk, at least a little bit.

In so doing, I found out that the real me was really a square. I also discovered a sense of relief in being a square publicly. I could say I liked the academic dean, and that I enjoyed his company. I could say I enjoyed the *Reader's Digest*, or just sitting in the yard, listening to a baseball game. There were some things about the "establishment" I enjoyed. It felt good to be able to say so.

I could say that I liked cleanliness and neatness. I was opposed to drugs. I could like my books in order, my yard mowed and trimmed, my files put away systematically, and my desk cleaned off. It came slowly. But I did reach the point where I could say, "I'm a square. It's all right to be a square; I can even like myself as a square." Some of my friends gave me curious looks at times, but they were still my friends. They did not disapprove of me.

One reason my friends gave me curious looks was that they could now see a difference in my behavior, but they did not know why. With one or two exceptions, they did not know what I was going through.

For I was still going through *it*.

I was learning about myself, I was getting in touch with my feelings, and I was learning a little bit about being me. But I was still hurting. Badly. My stomach was still knotted up and flip-flopping. Each morning, I doubted if I could get through the day. I sat alone and wept a good deal of the time. What I was learning about myself, my past, and being me was not yet eliminating my problem. Or even lessening it.

Five

*L*earning about myself, my past, and being me was a very important thing *for the long haul.* It was very constructive as a path to a healthier way of life. But I was still suffering too much to be patient or to take the long-term view.

I was still distracted and shaken much of the time. I could rarely concentrate. When preparing lecture notes, I often had to read, and then reread, the same passage several times. Only then would my mind register what I was reading.

In conversations, I had the same concentration problem. Even as I talked with someone, my mind would snap off on its own and seize on some terrible projection: I was going to die! . . . I was going to fall apart completely! or something similar. As a result, I often lost my train of thought completely while I was conversing. Sometimes it would happen while I was speaking, other times while I was listening. I was in lots of conversations that I could not reconstruct ten minutes later.

In addition to the panic and the terror, I had strong feelings of self-disgust. I didn't like myself for having those feelings. Having so much fear, for no reason that I could see, disgusted me. I saw myself as an incompetent, inept, human being. I was unworthy; I couldn't even control my day-to-day feelings as most people could. I saw myself as a big baby. My self-disgust did not help my situation of course; it made it worse.

Because the problem persisted on this acute level, I had to fight back somehow. I needed relief. Fast relief, not long-term, and I needed weapons to fight with.

So I began to develop some. I fought back with every weapon I could find and develop. I became the faculty advisor to the student newspaper and worked long hours at the job. I continued to give my students extra writing projects that were little work for them, but a great deal for me. I needed as much busywork as possible, for free time or time alone terrified me.

At home, I was hungry for wood-cutting, snow-shoveling, and the like. I plunged into whatever task there was to do and worked my way through it. I cleaned house. I did the dishes and vacuumed the rugs. I dusted the furniture. Many times I just wanted to lie down and cry and give up and let the world go ahead without me. But I never did.

I was learning the weapon of "losing myself." I was learning how to get so absorbed in an activity that I could temporarily escape my problem.

Athletics became a very important weapon. Sports had always been important to me, but never so much as they were now. I began to go to every athletic event at our college that I could. I went to basketball games, soccer games, wrestling matches, and baseball games. At basketball games, I yelled and hollered and managed to get away from myself for a couple of hours. When the game was over, the feelings of terror came rushing back, but I was learning how to escape, if only for an hour or two.

I could do somewhat the same thing by watching sports on television, but the element of crowd enthusiasm was always missing. Without the crowd, it just wasn't the same absorbing experience. I was soon "the regular" at nearly all the college sports events. I hardly missed a one.

I began participating in sports more than I ever had in my life. A close friend, who taught P.E., invited me to join his jogging class. I quickly accepted, although at any other time in my life, I would have received an invitation to a jogging class with no enthusiasm.

Shortly after the beginning of the semester, in mid-February, when my despair was most acute, I became a jogger. I remember pounding along snow-packed streets, wearing borrowed sweat clothes. Our course was about a mile and a half. I was weary and bleary-eyed, following sleepless nights, but I managed to finish the running course just like everyone else. And I found that while I was running, draining myself physically, I could shove my feelings of panic into the background. I was learning, first hand, the close connection between body and mind.

As the jogging class progressed, our running course was systematically lengthened. Soon it was two miles. Then three miles. Before long, I could run a three-mile course without getting tired. I could run a two-mile course in twelve minutes.

Our running course took us through a seminary campus, which was wooded and scenic. The campus also had a small lake. It was a beautiful course for running, and before too long, I was able to become completely absorbed in the experience. My fears and panic were put aside. Unfortunately, though, running class always ended. And when it did, my fears began crawling around inside of me again.

I took up the game of racquetball, which I had never played before. We had a new fieldhouse facility on our campus, with outstanding athletic resources. Nobody used them more than I did. There was even a faculty locker room. It became like my second home.

Racquetball is an intense, absorbing game, one of fast action and almost perpetual motion. It was precisely the kind of weapon for which I was looking. I could become deeply involved in the game and forget my troubles. I began playing at least one hour a day, slipping into the gym just after breakfast to reserve my court for the afternoon. There were many racquetball players on campus, among the students and the faculty. It was always easy to find opponents.

Some days, I played for two hours instead of one. By the end of the semester, I was a very good racquetball player. There were very few people who could beat me. I got little fulfillment personally, however, from winning at racquetball. The game was offering me an escape; and that was what I wanted from it. It was like jogging—a weapon.

Still another physical outlet was the faculty basketball team. We had about two games a week of full-court, fast-break basketball. So it was not uncommon for me to run two or three miles late in the morning, play racquetball for an hour in the early afternoon, and then play an intramural basketball game around supper time. Emotionally, I might have been coming apart. Physically, I was getting into great shape.

Because of all this strenuous exercise and my inability to eat, I began to wonder how much my body could endure. Within the span of six weeks, I had dropped from 180 pounds to 150. My body was often exhausted from lack of sleep. My eyes were sore with tiredness.

At six feet tall and only 150 pounds, I was so skinny that most of my clothes no longer fit me. My shirt collars were all loose at the neck and my pants had to be cinched up tightly at the waist. Whenever I felt any appetite at all, I quickly stuffed something fattening into my mouth—a donut, a milk shake, a candy bar. I was burning up so many calories a day I was desperate to put some back. It began to scare me, the way my weight was decreasing.

Even though I was concerned, however, the net effect was probably good. I was strong, and I had a tremendous endurance capacity. My goal was not to get into shape, just to get away from myself and my fears. But I could not help getting lean and hard—it just happened.

I was still experiencing dizzy spells, mostly at school. They occurred in the hallways, on the stairs, and sometimes while I was teaching classes. Judy had been urging me for some time to see a doctor; not only in connection with the dizzy spells, but also to find out if the emotional disorder that was plaguing me might have a physiological origin. I had consistently procrastinated. The thought of going to a doctor frightened me; I was afraid that an examination might reveal an additional problem. This was a childish attitude, but I found that my terror was spreading; at first it was free-floating and nameless, but now I was terrified by whatever life could offer that was unusual or unpredicted.

Finally, I consented to go to the doctor. We did not have a family doctor, so I went to Dr. Green on the advice of one of my colleagues. Dr. Green was a small, thin man in his sixties, with a finely-honed wit, and a shock of unruly white hair.

His office and reception room were located on the first floor of his home, a large, white frame house. He asked me a number of questions about my health history and wrote the answers in a folder. Then he asked me why I had come for an examination. Summarizing as well as I could, I told him of my terror and of the breakdown I had gone through and was still suffering from. I told him of my experience at the mental health unit. He puffed on his pipe thoughtfully and made an occasional note.

He gave me a simple, conventional examination in his office, and then gave me an EKG. Then he took my blood pressure. I was sitting on the edge of the examination table as he pumped up the cuff and then studied the reading. He studied it closely, and then pumped up again and released it slowly. Still not satisfied, he went and closed the door which led to the reception room. Then he pumped up the cuff again and gave it his closest attention as he released it.

"Stand up," he commanded. Now I was afraid. I stood up, and he pumped and released twice.

"Now lie down." I lay down on the table and the doctor took two more readings. I was very much afraid.

Finally, he put his stethoscope away and re-lit his pipe. "Have you ever had high blood pressure before?"

"No," I answered quickly. "Never. Is it high?"

"I get a reading of 150 over 100. That's high."

"Is it bad?"

"It's not terrible, but it's too high. Especially that lower reading; it's too high."

He took my blood pressure one more time, then went back to his desk and made some more notes in his folder.

He puffed on his pipe and made some checkmarks on a printed form. "I want you to have these tests done tomorrow morning at the hospital. You should be there at about eight o'clock in the morning. Take this form with you. Tonight, you have to fast. Nothing to eat after six P.M. Then, nothing to eat or drink before the blood tests are done in the morning. Do you understand?"

"Yes."

"Nothing to eat or drink after six P.M. tonight. Remember."

I went home, my stomach constricted with fright.

My fears accompanied me to the hospital the following morning. I sat in the waiting room, holding the slip of paper in my hands. I felt a terrible discouragement. I was thrust into absolute terror by any event in my life that deviated from the norm. I recognize now that I was fighting to structure my life totally, so that I would never have to experience any deviations. I realized with a great sadness that something was seriously wrong with me, and I had no solution.

Finally, it was my turn. Technicians took several blood samples from my arm. When they were finished, they told me, "We'll send these results to Dr. Green in a day or two. He'll probably call you when he gets them."

In a little less than a week, Dr. Green called me and I went to his office. Immediately, he took my blood pressure. He took it while I was standing, sitting, and then lying down. He went to his desk and made some notes again. "It's still high," he said. "150 over 100."

"It's probably just my tension that's causing it," I said, trying to minimize.

"Maybe. Is that what you'd like to think?"

I looked down; I felt discovered. "Yes, I guess it is."

"Why?"

"I don't want to think that there's anything else wrong with me."

"Well, you may be right. Your tests don't show any problems. If you are suffering from acute anxieties, it's not from any physiological cause."

"What should I do?" I asked.

"I'll make you three or four suggestions. I'll prescribe you a mild valium; it will help you sleep. Take a glass of wine in the evening. And take it easy. Calm down. You're too young to be suffering like this."

I felt ashamed and discouraged.

He went on, "For your blood pressure problem, I want to give you a diet that's low in salt and fat. I have one printed that I'll give you. Don't put any salt on your food. No salt at all, O.K.?"

"O.K."

"Come back in about three months, and we'll check your blood pressure again."

We shook hands, and I left. Naturally, I was very

afraid. If my emotions were driving my blood pressure up, why not a stroke? Why not a heart attack? Out of fear, I began monitoring my blood pressure. I had it checked nearly every day by the college nurse.

I took the valium at night, but it did not help me sleep. One night I took a double dose and found that I slept a little bit, but felt very woozy and groggy the next day. So I gave up on the pills altogether.

I continued to run and play basketball and racquetball. I had not told Dr. Green about my athletic activities, fearing he might tell me to quit on account of my blood pressure.

At about this time, I began reading self-help books, one after the other. My awareness of how much people are hurting was expanded as I visited the self-help section of local book stores. There was row after row of books on changing one's attitude, one's looks, one's beliefs, one's relationships, one's sex life, one's success ratio, one's very existence. People are hurting; they want happiness.

I was hurting. I wanted happiness. I can't begin to remember all the books I read, but I do remember more than one book by Norman Vincent Peale, including *The Power of Positive Thinking*. I read several other books of Christian reassurance. I read Eric Berne and Erich Fromm. I read *I'm Okay, You're Okay*. I read many other psychology books. Some were lightweight, and some were heavyweight.

It would be more accurate to say that I *devoured* those books than to say that I read them. I tore into them. I was desperate. Like most people who suffer, I wanted a way out. I wanted an answer, and I wanted it right away. Many of the books spoke with such assurance, and voiced so little in the way of doubt, that I kept thinking I *was* going to find a quick and easy answer. So much of that kind of literature told me what I wanted to hear: that I could see my life change quickly and easily. "If you open your heart to Jesus, your problems will vanish." Or, "If you just follow these few simple steps, you can change your life." Those were the kinds of statements I often read and wanted to hear.

Some of the authors I have mentioned do not pretend that there are simple answers to complex problems. Yet, "simple answer" literature was what I wanted, and I often used it as a temporary weapon.

Even though many of the books I read were superficial, those by psychologists and religious leaders alike, they had a beneficial effect. I often saw in such books how others had suffered, just as I was suffering, and yet survived. It always seemed to help to know that others had endured what I was going through, and worse. The absolute certainty of Norman Vincent Peale inspired me with determination more than once. "Trust in God," he said. "And take one day at a time." I tried to heed his advice.

The warm assurance of Leslie Weatherhead had the same kind of positive effect on me, and so did the enthusiasm of Thomas Kelley. Superficial psychology books could have the same kind of pumping-up effect: "You can be the person you want to be; all you have to do is make up your mind." After reading the right sentence or paragraph, I could often begin a day all fired-up with determination, like an athlete psyched up for the big game.

One particularly helpful book, with reference to concentration, was a book called *You Must Relax*, by a physician named Dr. Edmund Jacobson. Dr. Jacobson outlines a technique for systematically relaxing the body and putting it at complete rest. That kind of material was very important to me, because I was having so much difficulty concentrating. It seemed that I had to retrain myself in the skill of concentration. Fear would well up inside me and then my mind would race out of control, jumping from one fearful possibility to another. Most of those "fearful possibilities" were things that would probably never happen, or things that weren't fearful at all, even if they did happen. It was as if the fear would attack my stomach, and then my mind would race around frantically, trying to find a target for the fear.

I needed some control. I needed some skills to help me exert some control over my own thoughts and feelings. I knew by this point that I had never been good at concentration. I had always been jittery and unskilled at relaxing or focusing. Previous to my current struggle, though, my anxious tendencies had always stayed within "normal" boundaries. My defense mechanisms, like everyone else's, had been strong enough to screen out excessive fears and apprehensions. Thus, in trying to learn relaxation techniques and concentration techniques, I was trying to overcome a pattern of a lifetime, not merely a pattern of a few weeks.

Those were some of the survival weapons I was learning to use. My *coping* weapons—spectator sports, running, racquetball, basketball, self-help books, and relaxation techniques—these were the things that were helping to get me from one day to the next. And if my suffering was not abating, at least I was encouraged by my own determination to fight back.

There was one very precious morning at about this time that provided me with special encouragement. One cold, clear morning at the end of February, just before sunrise, Jason came toddling into our bedroom. We had celebrated his first birthday just two weeks earlier. I sat on the edge of the bed, and he sat on a small stool; together we watched out our east window as the sun slowly rose along the ridge across the road. Together we watched the sky lighten, then saw the sun itself peek above the ridge and lighten the snow and bare trees on the western slope.

I looked at him, and he looked at me, and we smiled.

We were sharing a precious moment, and it filled me with hope. I vowed that whatever it was I was suffering through, *I would never give in to it.*

Six

*A*t the same time I was developing the weapons that gave me something in the way of immediate relief, I was also developing something that would prove to be of more lasting value: a life of Christian faith.

A life of prayer, a life of faith? Those were things I had never really tried before. At least, I had never tried them in any serious way. As a minister's son, I had grown up in the church, gone regularly to Sunday school and church youth groups. I did not like church. Growing up in a parsonage, I felt that church activities were forced upon me, and I was resentful. I envied my friends, most of whom were free to come and go from church as they pleased. As a kid, I remember being teased for being a minister's son. I used to "act up" or clown around in response to this kidding, to mask the hurt and embarrassment I felt. My association with the church was not something I cherished. By junior high school, I was thinking of ways to skip out, and by senior high school, I was skipping out. I had several friends who were also forced to go to Sunday school. We used to meet at the church and then leave; we spent our Sunday mornings at a truck stop, drinking coffee and talking together.

After high school, for the next twelve years or so I rejected religion and religious institutions. During that period of time, I was always in a college environment, either as a student or as a teacher. I was in the humanities, where the prevailing attitude about religious faith and churches was a negative one. Churches were superstitious refuges for small-minded people. In graduate school, too, most of my peers dismissed religion as something for the intellectually impoverished. It was the perfect ongoing atmosphere to harden my attitudes against religious faith and the church. The sum of my attitude was even more understandable because I had always been a person who was easily influenced and led by the opinions of others. In the anti-war movement, it was easy to continue rejecting the church as just one of many outmoded establishments.

So, starting a life of prayer was not an easy thing for me to do. But I had to try. My resources were not sufficient to conquer my crippling fears. Neither were the human resources I was trying. I needed God.

I had made my first cry for help to human agencies and human knowledge. My second cry for help went, instead, to Jesus Christ. When I started to pray, I took my most important first step toward a life of fulfillment.

Those first prayers were ones of desperation and disbelief: "Why? Why, God, why is this thing happening to me? Have I done something wrong or evil? Is this a punishment?" I gushed out to God all my fear and despair. I pleaded with Him to deliver me from my suffering. I reminded Him that I might be losing my mind and that I didn't know if I could survive. I asked Him if Satan had a hand in causing my problems. If so, I begged God to drive Satan out of my life. These were cries of grief as much as they were prayers, but they were a beginning.

They were also honest and real, with no guard up and no pretense. Just as we often are in our personal relationships, we can be pretentious and dishonest in prayer. But if those early prayers of mine were essentially just desperate cries for help, they were one hundred percent honest.

I went off by myself into the fields in the early morning and late at night, in the cold, the snow, and the wind. I poured out my fears to God. I asked Him to help me. I asked Him to help me have a personal relationship with Jesus Christ.

Earlier, I mentioned Dick Dutton had given me the little book that many have read and cherished—John Baillie's *Diary of Private Prayer*. Each morning I read one of the meditations and asked God to go with me throughout the day. At night, I read another meditation and prayed for help. Out of that experience I usually got some feeling of reassurance and hope. It was, I feel, an important second step: I was inviting God into my life every day.

During the day, I would repeat the Lord's Prayer from time to time, or I would close my office door and say the twenty-third Psalm several times over. "The Lord is my shepherd: I shall not want"(v. 1 KJV). The words provided me with a surge of hope. The Lord was *my* shepherd too; He would not abandon me, He would not leave me alone. "Yea, though I walk through the valley of the shadow of death, I will fear no evil . . ."(v. 4 KJV).

I had dug out of a desk drawer a very small red-letter New Testament that my father had given me in 1951. It was small enough to fit into my pocket, and I began to carry it with me. Each day I gathered hope from various passages in the Bible that encouraged me. A particularly helpful passage was Matthew 6:33–34, where Jesus reminded His listeners to "seek ye first the kingdom of God and his righteousness, and all these things shall be added unto you"(v.33 KJV). This passage spoke clearly to me. If I wanted to survive and overcome, I needed to seek the Lord.

Also, I identified with the occasion in the temple when Jesus cast out the demons from a man who suffered possession. After reading that passage, I usually prayed for God to cast out my demons. Another passage I read frequently for help was the occasion when Jesus calmly took time for the children: "Suffer little children to come unto me, and forbid them not: for of such is the kingdom of God"(Mark 10:14; Luke 18:16 KJV). That passage spoke to me because I felt like a little child in need of help. In truth, I was coming to God like a little child, helpless and confused. Time and again, the life of Jesus, perfect in its calm, peace, and purpose, lifted me up.

At about that same time, we started going to church. Dick Dutton had invited us to a "house church" he was leading—an informal, interdenominational group worship.

For a few months previous, Judy and I had been doing a little church shopping. It may have been the birth of Jason that got us interested in attending church. I'm not sure. We had visited a Unitarian church, a Methodist church, and an Episcopalian church. All three were in large old church buildings with big sanctuaries but had very small attendance. The congregations seemed to have few young people and little vitality. No doubt at one time they had been thriving and active churches, but no longer. We could not get enthused about any of them.

How different it was at the house church! I remember the first morning we went—a bitter cold, raw morning in late February. My troubles had by this time persisted for nearly seven weeks.

House church met at the Dutton home, a plain, old two-story frame house. Worship was conducted in the living room, a very plain room. Including the children, there were about thirty or so people there. During worship, some were sitting in chairs, some were sitting on the floor, and some were even standing. There were about twelve to fourteen families involved.

Several of the people there were rough, unpolished working people. I was surprised because I had assumed that such a "religious experiment" would be dominated by intellectuals. I could not have been more wrong. The house church membership cut across religious, economic, and social lines.

There were teachers, counselors, working class people, and the unemployed. There were housewives, working women, the young and the old. It was truly a mixed group, consisting of Baptists, Methodists, Catholics, and Christian Jews.

What was dominant at house church was love, for Christ and for other people. We felt, as newcomers, immediate acceptance and caring. We sang, that first morning, old hymns like "Amazing Grace" and folk hymns like "We are One in the Spirit." Dick Dutton accompanied on his guitar, strumming a few basic chords.

A black teen-aged boy, who was a foster care child of one of the house church couples, played a solo on the guitar. He stumbled over a few of the notes and had to start over once or twice, but everyone applauded warmly when he was finished. They genuinely supported his effort. It was the great strength of house church, that *every single person* felt cared for.

That first morning, there was a period of time given over to sharing. People in the group shared their feelings, their problems, and their faith. They asked for advice, and they asked for good listeners.

Later, Dick played the guitar again, and we all sang "He's Got the Whole World in His Hands." During the singing, the whole group honored our little son, Jason, by singing a verse: "He's got Jason in His hands." I fought back tears of joy as Jason toddled around on the floor, beaming as he listened to their singing. It exhilarated me to see this group of people affirm my little boy, who meant so much to me.

I felt a great flood of joy that morning. It was not my "Road to Damascus." My life was not instantly changed or turned around. My problems did not disappear. But I was taking an important step along the road to real faith in Jesus Christ, the step of meaningful group worship.

That particular morning, though, I wasn't thinking in terms of steps. I was relishing the experience of house church. It was an experience that filled me with warmth and hope. In fact, *hope* is the key word; for several weeks I had felt hopeless, filled with despair. The world had become such a frightening place—and the fright had burst upon me so unexpectedly. That morning at house church, though, I found something else I had not expected—human love, freely given.

Judy and I were thrilled with our first house church experience. She, too, was feeling anxiety and discouragement. The house church came as a source of hope. We began attending house church regularly, and I think it helped me carry on my fight more than anything else I was doing. House church was always informal and intimate. There was always time to deal with each person's needs. As a result, morning worship at house church often lasted two hours or longer. I felt accepted and loved. So did Judy and Jason. We were being cared for, and we were helping to care for others. To do something for someone else—to help another person figure out a problem— that was very important to me.(In group therapy the members were to help each other, too, but there was not the sense of true compassion among the participants.)

I felt so worthless during those days that I did not feel qualified to help someone else. I was so unable to run my own life, I didn't feel I deserved the chance to help someone else with his or her needs. But in house church, I felt accepted just the way I was, and people asked for my help. That helped me begin to see myself again as a person of value, not a worthless freak.

Gradually, we got to know and love our fellow house church members.

There was Karen, a young woman who was in the process of losing her eyesight. She was a diabetic. When we met Karen, she was almost totally blind. She called herself the "Baptist Jew." She had been raised in a Jewish home, and had later converted to Christianity and become a Baptist. Now she was a member of house church.

It was very difficult for Karen to accept her blindness. She had been to see surgeons and eye specialists even when it seemed hopeless. She was grieving and angry.

"Department of Family Services sent a woman out to our house on Tuesday," she told us one Sunday morning. "She is supposed to be a specialist in living skills and home care."

"Was she able to help you?" Dick Dutton asked.

"I don't know," she answered. Karen was a pretty woman, with regular features and long black hair, carefully styled. "I don't know why they sent her."

"What did she help you with?"

"Oh, she helped me with cooking things. She was showing me how to cook on a stove by touch. How to store things by touch."

"That sounds pretty good," said Dick. "What else?"

"She showed me how to store cleaning supplies and utensils by touch." Karen was not enjoying this and was bitter about it. Softly, she began to cry. "I can't even cook . . . or clean. . . . I wonder what good I am." She sobbed softly and continued, "I don't know if my socks match . . . I can't even put on my make-up." She sobbed so hard that she had to stop speaking. She was humiliated and miserable.

The house church members supported her and prayed

with her from week to week. Department of Family Services kept sending personnel to visit her, and eventually she adjusted to the idea of receiving help. One Sunday morning she showed us how she had learned to apply her lipstick, using a touch method. We gave her a round of applause and a big hug. Karen's suffering made me ashamed of my own. Why should I be so inept as to suffer without a real crisis, while she struggled with such a real one? Karen was hanging by her fingernails. As far as I am concerned, she was, and is, a real heroine. Our world is full of heroes, and we don't even know who they are. Karen is an unproclaimed heroine, possessing great courage and determination; such people are all around us, yet we don't know who they are.

House church was helping Karen, just as it was helping me. It was vital for Karen to receive the ongoing support of the body of Christ; her daughters were troubled by their mother's suffering. Her husband was mystified and threatened. He had a modest income from a job in a grocery store, and Karen's trips to specialists were building a large medical debt.

Gertrude was another member of house church who needed our care. She was a middle-aged woman who had lived as a single parent for a number of years. She had a teenaged son and a very modest income from her job. Her son was rebellious, and getting into drugs. Gertrude was not an assured or assertive person, and she felt inadequate to guide her son through this period of his life. She felt very separated from him, as if a gulf were opening between her son and herself. She said he needed a father to relate to. She was very troubled.

Gertrude was a timid person who was often intimidated. She told us a story one morning in house church. She had been driving back from a town further upstate in New York the week before and had run out of gas on a country road. It was a lonely place in the road, and it would soon be getting dark; she was afraid. She began walking and finally came to a house at the edge of a village, at dusk. It turned out that the home was that of the local Presbyterian minister, who drove her to a gas station, and then to her car, and helped her get on her way again. As Gertrude told this story, tears formed in her eyes. "That was God looking out for me, " she said softly. "God was guiding me to that place so that I could find help. That was God," she repeated.

For a moment, no one spoke. Then Dick said softly, "That is the simplest faith. It is like the faith of a child. It is faith that is childlike, and Jesus reminds us many times to be as little children."

Ben, another of our members, was a single young man. He was shy and did not have social skills. He had a high school diploma, but he had trouble finding a job and then keeping it. He needed guidance and kindness on the job. Most jobs did not give him those courtesies. Most of us at house church helped him to find the right job and to keep it. We often prayed with him.

The longer I was associated with house church, the more I understood the meaning of trust. I shared my problems. I shared what I was going through—the fear and the terror. I was willing to risk exposing myself. I felt acceptance, love, and support. House church was human beings in ministry to one another out of love. In house church I learned the meaning of supportive, Christian caring, of Christian community.

I also began to understand how any Christian church has the potential to rediscover and experience real Christian community. Acts 2:46–47 outlines this need clearly: "And day by day, attending the temple together and breaking bread in their homes, they partook of food with glad and generous hearts, praising God and having favor with all the people" (RSV). Here indeed is the standard for real Christian community, a community that is open to the deepest kind of sharing, creating the deepest, most trusting kinds of relationships. It is a place where Christian love is freely given and freely received—a place where trust is so strong that people are willing to risk, to drop their guard, and to reveal their most private concerns and joys to one another.

I began to understand that the resource necessary to create and maintain this kind of community was the love of God, revealed in Jesus Christ. For those who have experienced that love, there is the urge to share it or, in the words of the folk hymn, to "pass it on." The Christian community can be built upon the foundation of the greater love, that deeper love, the love of Christ.

It even occurred to me that this may truly be the meaning of the phrase, the kingdom of God: Christian people in the Christian community, ministering to one another on the deepest level, fueled by the love of God.

One of the things, of course, that I had been trying to learn was "getting in touch with my feelings." House church was helping me do that and to share those feelings. Naturally, this was difficult for me, as it is for most people. In our culture we do not live in a spirit of trust and openness, and I am a product of our culture, just like everybody else. But in house church, I saw a better kind of community. I felt loved and cared for. My family felt loved and cared for. I was experiencing the joy of loving and caring for others.

I should point out that the house church family was not without conflicts. Anywhere that people interact, there will be some conflict. There was some disagreement among house church adults, for example, about children's activities. We had several young and pre-school children, and some of the adults felt that they should be entertained elsewhere for at least a part of the worship experience. Others felt this would be inappropriate—it wasn't like house church to follow the conventional structures. Separating the young from the old was not consistent with our philosophy. A kind of compromise was developed to solve this problem: the children had their own church school experience for a part of the morning, then they shared with us during the rest of our worship.

Some were concerned about "outreach" or "mission." They felt that mission was such a vital part of the Christian faith that we should do more in that area. Others felt that our ministry to one another was so important that we should take care to preserve it, even if we did increase our involvement in outreach. We gradually increased our mission projects; we began to help with the Peace Meals program for the elderly, and we began planning a Christian coffee house for young people. I remember one very special day when the members of house church spent the day picking apples together. Afterwards, we made batches of applesauce that we donated to the Peace Meals program.

Our disagreements never got bitter. Nobody was hardened to anybody else. We trusted and cared for each other. We could handle disagreements.

Through house church, Judy and I formed some deep and lasting friendships. I spent more and more time with Dick Dutton. He was building a new home, which he hoped to move into by summer. On several occasions I helped him with the work. Usually I wanted the work for therapeutic reasons, and to have time with him; he was aware of this but was always glad to have my help.

Late one afternoon in April, after the two of us had established a strong relationship, we were working together on his house. It was late enough in the afternoon that it was beginning to get dark, and there was a chill in the air. We took a break and sat beside each other. The new house was on a bluff in the country. The studs were framed up, but no walls were yet in place, and we could look off across the fields and the sections of timber. It was peaceful and beautiful, and I felt very close to Dick at that moment.

"How are you doing these days?" he asked me quietly.

"I'm grinding it out," I said.

"Are you still hurting?"

I nodded my head. "I'm afraid so."

"Are you making any progress?"

I shook my head no; even as I began to think about my anxiety attacks, my stomach constricted tight with fear. Wretchedly, I looked at what should have been a marvelous moment; the nearness of a dear friend, the joy of hard work shared together, and the beauty of the surroundings. I felt only fear and frustration. "I am still trying to get to the bottom of this, Dick," I said. "If it goes on much longer, I don't think I can survive it."

"As far as I can see," he said quietly, "you're doing everything you can do."

"That's what scares me," I said. "I'm doing everything I can do, and the problem's not getting solved. I may be doing everything I can do, but I'm not doing the right thing. If I were, I would be getting to the bottom of this."

"Not necessarily," he said. "Everything you're doing may be of great benefit somewhere down the road."

Frustrated, I said, "Dick, I don't live somewhere down the road. I live in the here and now, just like everybody else. I need an answer, and I need it now, not somewhere down the road."

"Sometimes I think you're too compulsive about finding the answer. Getting to the bottom of it, as you put it."

"Dick, that's easy for you to say. It's easy for anyone to say who's not going through this."

He looked at me with compassion. "I'm not trying to

minimize what you're going through; not for a moment. I just think sometimes you might make more progress if you just let go, instead of fighting to get an answer all the time."

"I'd love to take that advice; I really would."

"But you're not going to, are you?"

"I doubt it. I don't think I can."

We sat for some time, silently, watching dusk settle down over the fields and the hills. It was getting chillier. I wanted to ask him about his faith, and I finally worked up the courage.

"Would you tell me about your faith?" I asked quietly, not looking at him.

"What do you want to know?"

"When you speak with God, what is it like?"

He pulled his knees up under his chin and hooked his arms around his legs. He smiled. "Sometimes when I'm alone with God, I feel His presence," he said. "Just like the presence of a person. It's not a body, or a face, or anything like that. It's just a presence; a very real, warm, wonderful communion. I feel filled up with joy and hope."

"And?"

"And I just keep still and listen. Not for words, but just to listen with my heart. It is more wonderful than anything else in the world I have ever known."

"Does God give you advice?"

"Not in words; He doesn't speak to me with words. But when I feel myself in His presence, I start to see things more clearly. Everything seems to get in focus, and the things I should be doing are clear to me."

I envied him terribly at the way he was so in touch with himself and with the Lord. I wanted to be in touch with myself, and I wanted to be in touch with God the way he was. I felt like such a beginner as a Christian. "Dick," I blurted out, "do you think God is causing me to go through these things? Does He want me to suffer like this?"

"No, I don't," said Dick quickly. "I don't believe God wants you to suffer. It may be, though, that God wants you to serve Him."

"Do you think I could?"

"Of course. You love other people. But you must find a way to respect yourself, you simply must."

I wanted to, but I did not feel as if I could help myself. I felt very weak, not strong.

Dick Dutton and I had many more conversations about the Christian faith, during the weeks of early spring. He was, and is, as fine a Christian as I have ever known. He has a zest for living and a deep sensitivity to the needs of others. He encouraged me at all times not to give up and to grow in the faith.

Late in April, Dick encouraged Judy and me to go to a Christian workshop in Washington, D.C. It was one of the *Serendipity* workshops presented by the Lyman Coleman organization. Dick had a difficult job convincing me to go, because I was so rigidly attached to the predictable routines and activities I depended on to fight off anxiety attacks. He kept urging me, however, and I finally consented. Judy and I both went, along with Dick and another dear friend from house church, Rich DeGeus.

The workshop was held in the Sheraton Hotel ballroom in D.C. There were four hundred participants. After breakfast, we all gathered for opening hymns and prayers. We were then separated into groups of eight, and I was separated from Judy, Dick, and Rich for the rest of the day. By design, each of us was placed in a group of strangers.

There were two men and five women in my group. We each had a *Serendipity* workbook, and we were led through a series of nonthreatening questions and exercises, which were designed to put us in touch with the other members of our group. For instance, we read the Scripture passage where Jesus invited Peter to walk on the water (see Matt. 14:22–36), and then we were asked what we would have done in that position. Would we have run the other way? Discussed the matter? Jumped into the water and swam out to Jesus? Walked bravely out to meet Jesus, as He had commanded?

As the day wore on, I found that all the members of my group, other than myself, were clergy or people in church vocations of one kind or another. One was a priest. One was a nun. Another was a church education specialist, another a minister, and soon on.

By afternoon, our sharing had become deep enough that our masks were gone. Our facades had melted away, and we had become open, honest, and trusting people. The priest shared that he seemed to be losing his faith. He was in his late fifties, and he was deeply troubled that his faith, which had governed his life for so many years, might be evaporating.

The young woman who was the church education specialist had a daughter with club feet, a hole in her heart, and curvature of the spine. Most of the girl's life had been spent recuperating from one operation or another, and she was lonely. The woman wept continually as she told us of her struggle to help her daughter and to accept these difficulties herself.

Late in the afternoon, the group wanted to know about my breakdown. I told them in summary, without fear. I felt so very close to every one of them that I wanted to tell them what I had been going through. When I had finished telling them about the breakdown, the therapy, and all the fears, Pam, the nun, reached over and put her hand on top of mine. She looked me straight in the eye and said quietly, "For the next year, I will pray for you every night at Vespers. Every night at seven, look at the clock and know that I will be praying for you. God will not leave you to suffer forever." She spoke so simply, and directly from her heart, that I found my eyes filling with tears. I squeezed her hand.

When the day was ended, our group embraced. There were tears and laughter. Each of us placed a cross around the neck of the group member nearest, in an act of consecration as we went our separate ways.

I got back together with Dick, Rich, and Judy. Their experiences had been as wonderful as mine. We held each other and laughed together. Each of us wore our cross joyfully.

Rich's face was shining. "How was it for you?" I asked him.

"I'll be honest with you," he said, smiling. "I didn't even want to come to this thing. I thought it would be people manipulating people, playing games with them." Then he smiled very broadly. "But I was wrong. This was wonderful. I've never been so touched by anything." Then he and I embraced one another.

I cherished that day for months and years. It showed me once again how many people are hurting desperately, and how much they long to share their suffering with Christian listeners. This fact was becoming clearer and clearer to me. We all hurt. We all want to risk ourselves and enter deeply into a sharing relationship, but we don't know how. We haven't learned how. Instead, we pay a professional listener, usually called a therapist, and let it go at that.

My *Serendipity* experience also affirmed to me that we were on the right track in the house church family. We were building trust and love—the most authentic kind of Christian community. Judy's own Christian faith, long dormant, was being reawakened. House church was for her a joyous experience. All the pain I was experiencing was also a threat to her, and house church was a substantial source of help for her.

I remember vividly how, when we arrived back home from D.C., I went outside and sat on the stone fence in our yard. It was a still, cold night with a sky full of stars. I thanked God for the experience of the *Serendipity* workshop, and I thanked Him for the house church family. I felt a special peace and joy settle down upon me. I asked God to enter my life and take it over; for I understood that if I had Him at the center of my life, He would displace the neurotic disorder that was lurking there now. I sat for some time with that understanding clearly before me.

Seven

As the weeks went by, I continued to struggle. I was getting through each day, but not much more. I was running, reading, playing ball, going to group therapy, praying, and going to house church. It was not enough.

I was still not getting relief. Nothing was fast enough. The nights without sleep were ever with me, and I stumbled groggily through each subsequent day. I began to see little flashes of light around objects I looked at; a car would pass and I would see bright crackles of light radiating from it, as though I were looking into an exploding flashbulb. I was taking some blood pressure medication, and I called Dr. Green to see if I might be having a reaction to the medication. He said it would be possible, but not likely. I tried to dismiss the flashes of light as just another anxiety-related symptom that would disappear as soon as I got my problem solved.

Still, I was desperate to shake off those feelings of terror and panic. I was still mystified and angry. I still insisted that "this can't be happening to me!" On and on. Somehow, I had to "get to the bottom of it." I *had* to.

One afternoon later in April, Dick and I were working

on his house again. I told him how frustrated and desperate I was.

He put aside his hammer and wiped his hands on his nail apron. "Is the group therapy helping you at all?"

"Not much," I said. "It isn't worthless, but I just can't get personal attention."

"Too many people with too many needs, I suppose?"

"Exactly. I still want to dig down into my problem until I get right to the root of it. In group therapy, we have to stay too much near the surface."

"Then I'd say you ought to have your own therapist. Why not go to private counseling?"

Surprisingly, it was what I had hoped he would say. "Is that your advice?" I asked.

"I can't see why not. You've tried everything else. I don't think you'll be satisfied until you sit down one on one with a trained therapist and see if you can get to the root of the problem."

"I'd really like to," I said. "I guess I'm afraid I can't afford it."

"I'm not sure you can afford not to," he said. He smiled gently at me. "Jim, you've got to do whatever you think will help you. Your eyes have dark shadows and a sunken look. You're practically a bag of bones. I can only say you have to do what you think will help."

"I'd like to go to a private therapist," I said quickly. "I guess I've been afraid to spend the money."

"If you had respect for yourself you wouldn't care about the money. You are worth it."

"I suppose so," I murmured, embarrassed. I felt like a child, the way I needed direction.

"Forget the money," he said urgently. "The money is not important, but your survival is. Whatever it costs, you are worth a lot more. You are suffering terribly every day. Do whatever it takes to get well."

"Whom should I go to?" I asked.

"There's a man named Dr. Perry," Dick said. "I'd recommend him."

"Dr. Perry?"

"Yes, he's worked with us a couple of times at *PATH*, and he's made a few referrals to us. He's a Ph.D. in psychology with a private practice in town. He's got many clients. I think he's alert and capable. Give him a call."

The following week, I began individual therapy with Dr. Perry. He was a handsome, quiet man in his middle thirties. He had black hair with a little gray at the temples. He dressed well. He was so composed that he intimidated me. He was the therapist, and I was the patient. The mental patient. It hurt so deeply to be a "mental patient." I was furious about it.

Dr. Perry's office had a reception room and a private office. In the private office, he sat in his swivel chair behind the desk, and I sat in an easy chair in front. Behind the desk were built-in book cases on two walls. There were tasteful beige carpeting and matching beige drapes. I saw him each Thursday evening and paid $35 per session. That worked out to $140 per month. I could afford it, but barely.

The first night, he took notes as I told him about my breakdown, how it had started, what my feelings were like, when they were most intense, how I had gone to the mental health unit. I told him about running, sports, reading, prayer, and house church.

He asked me a few simple questions about my childhood, my adolescence, my mother, my father, my sisters, my marriage, and my son.

I wanted to figure this thing out, I told him. I wanted an answer to what was happening to me.

"There may not be an answer," he said calmly.

I froze inside. "No answer? How could that be?" I asked.

"If you want a single event or a single cause, you may not find it."

"There has to be some reason!"

"Not necessarily reason, singular; maybe reasons, plural."

"All right, whatever," I said urgently. "I want the answer."

"And I can only repeat, you may never find the answer to satisfy you. We might not be able to pinpoint any one cause for your breakdown."

I was beginning to sweat. "Is that what I'm having? A breakdown?"

Dr. Perry dismissed the question with a wave of his hand. "Call it what you want—breakdown, attack, acute anxieties, whatever. The point is that it's a breakdown of your emotional patterns. It's an emotional disorder. It hurts, it's paralyzing, it's mystifying. The name you give it is not really important."

What he was telling me was close to the same thing that Sarah had told me at the mental health unit. "So what do I do?" I asked quietly.

"We don't know yet. We haven't figured that out yet. Why don't you quit trying to identify a single cause? Quit trying so desperately to pinpoint the cause. You might be suffering today because of many years of a certain pattern of emotional development."

"Do you think I can get well?"

"Yes, I do. You're intelligent, and you seem willing to work. That's very important. Knowledge is very helpful. We want you to reach the point where you know what you are fighting, instead of just fighting blindly."

After that first night, I felt a surge of hope. Dr. Perry was a bright man with lots of experience. I felt confident that we would get somewhere. Now I would begin making progress.

Another night, after I had told him how acute the terror was, he asked me quietly, "Have you ever thought that you may *want* those feelings?"

"*Want* them?" I blurted out. "You've got to be kidding!"

"No, I'm not kidding. Maybe you want to suffer."

"How could I possibly want them?" I protested. "They are tearing me apart!"

"I'm not sure exactly," he said calmly. "There may be something deep inside you, maybe in your subconscious, that needs those feelings."

I felt terribly frustrated and betrayed. Was he going to "maybe" me to death? "I just can't think of anything to say," I muttered.

"Somehow," he went on unruffled, "there's probably a pay-off. You're probably getting something out of this. I don't know just what. It may be pity, pity for yourself. Pity as a replacement for love. I don't know. That's what we're here to find out."

That was a difficult idea for me to swallow, and I struggled with it for a number of days. If I wanted to suffer, then I was guilty—as well as incompetent. Eventually I got used to the idea and tried to use it as a tool for understanding myself. Did I want all this suffering? Was some part of me getting a pay-off?

In my sessions with Dr. Perry, he reaffirmed that all of my symptoms—panicky stomach, insomnia, chronic uneasiness, sweaty palms—were characteristic of generalized anxiety disorder. He helped me understand more completely the nature of generalized anxiety. It wasn't a very serious sounding name, but it could be a very disabling disorder. People with generalized anxiety, he observed, could not effectively allay feelings of threat and anxiety; hence such people were often in acute discomfort.

He went on to assure me, however, that I would probably never lose my grip on reality. It was unlikely I would "fall apart" or be unable to function. I might experience chronic, diffuse apprehensiveness, but I was not psychotic. I could get better.

How had I gotten to this point? How had I grown and developed to become this kind of person? In therapy, I was able to find partial answers to those questions, as various insights came to the surface.

Early in life, I developed feelings of "not being good enough." I did not "measure up." My parents were perfectionists. They imposed upon themselves the highest possible standards, and it was only natural that they would impose the same kinds of standards upon their children.

My father was a highly successful minister. In every church he served, he was loved and revered for his conscientiousness and his dedication. He never let anything slip—he followed every task through to a satisfactory conclusion. He was active with the youth groups, the women's groups, the administrative groups, the hospitalized church members, and the shut-ins. He never did a job half way or left a detail uncovered.

His record of success was stunning. Had he wanted, he could have become a bishop. His capabilities were so widely acknowledged that one of his fellow ministers said once to me, "If our conference had a pope, your father would be it."

My mother's standards were no lower. She was the perfect minister's wife. She always kept an immaculate home, fed parsonage visitors royally, was a highly effective officer in many church groups, and had all the necessary social skills to deal with parishioners of all kinds. She was an asset to the church choir and could even play the piano.

Without meaning to create a negative situation, my parents placed high expectations upon me and my sisters. As a child, I was an achiever, but I was never "number one." I was good in sports, school, and music. I made good grades and won lots of ribbons from music contests. Yet I was not happy with the things I did or the results I got.

I can remember coming home with tests on which I had scored ninety percent. My mother would ask, "Why didn't you get one hundred?" She said this partly in jest, but my mind recorded the fact that I could have done better. Often my father made me do household chores a second or third time, to "get it right." He would stand and watch me until I had finished the chore to his satisfaction.

Later, I began doing poorer work in school, and I was in ongoing conflict with my parents about my schoolwork.

As I outlined my childhood for Dr. Perry, he tried to get me to see the relevance of it in terms of what I was now going through. "You're an uneasy person," he said to me. "You don't like yourself because you're not perfect. The things you do are not perfect. You can't succeed."

I thought of what Sarah had told me some time earlier at the mental health center.

"What do you mean, I can't succeed?" I asked.

"You learned from your parents that it's important to be perfect. Naturally, you can't be perfect. Therefore, you can't succeed. Any job you do could always be done better. You receive no satisfaction from the things you do, because you aren't perfect, and you receive no satisfaction from the person you are for the same reason. You have a neurotic fear of not measuring up."

"But if I've always been this way, why am I having these attacks now?" I asked.

"I'm not sure. Somehow you must have overloaded your circuits, over a long period of time."

"What does that mean?"

He smiled. "Maybe too much compulsive behavior for too long."

Fine, I thought to myself. I now knew I had a generalized anxiety disorder and that my childhood had helped me become a neurotic person. "But how am I going to get rid of this disorder?" I asked. "What should I do?"

"In what respect?" he asked.

"In any respect," I answered, frustrated. "In *every* respect. Should I jog? Play basketball? Pray? Meditate? Am I doing the best things I can be doing?"

"It sounds to me like you want a formula."

Now I was really irritated. "Call it anything you want. Formula, plan, guidelines, whatever you want to call it. Call it compulsive if you want. But I need a plan. I need to know what to do. I need to know which activities are better for me than others."

"Try to get your teeth out of it; let go of it, try to flow with life a little bit."

"You're saying you don't know. You don't know what I should do."

"I think you should stop planning what to do."

It always seemed to come back to not knowing. All the reading I had done, all the analysis I and analysts had done, had no answer for this simple question: what should I do?

I was surviving; I was getting through this day and the next day, but I had no idea how to solve the problem; neither, it seemed, did anybody else.

I found in personal analysis that I had always had nervous, compulsive tendencies, but those tendencies had always been within the boundaries of "normalcy." Now my feelings were out of bounds and out of control.

On another occasion, I told Dr. Perry how worthless I felt. I told him of my feelings of shame and incompetence. I was not able to control my feelings or simply live life the way normal people do.

"Those feelings are understandable, but have you ever thought of the pride you might have in yourself?"

"Pride? For what?"

"I'd say pride in your courage."

"You can call it courage if you want, but I'd rather get well."

He ignored me. "It takes courage for you to keep going every day," he said. "It takes a lot of courage. You should be proud; you have guts."

Maybe so, I thought, but I felt a lot more fear than pride.

Then he changed the subject. "I think you also need to start thinking about choosing. Remember when we talked about the possibility that you might want these feelings of suffering?"

"I remember," I said.

"You are making choices," he said. "It is my opinion that we choose our feelings; they are not something forced upon us. If a person makes you mad, he doesn't really make you mad, you choose to be mad. You understand?"

"I'm not sure," I said.

"Feelings don't just happen to us, like the flu. We choose them. It may not be obvious to us that we choose them, but I believe we still do. When I drive to the corner and choose to turn left or right, that's a choice that's pretty obvious to me. When I choose to get angry with somebody, I'm making a choice that's much more subtle, but I believe I'm still making a choice."

"I think I see," I said.

"For some reason, I believe you are choosing to be terrified. You are getting a pay-off somehow, and you are making a choice."

"So what should I do?"

"Start thinking about your choices. See if you can see feelings as something you choose, rather than as something that happens to you. Try some small ones at first, then work up."

"I think I see," I said.

"Think about it for a while."

"What you're saying is that if I'm the one choosing to have those feelings, then I have the power to *un*choose them."

"Exactly," said Dr. Perry. "It's very important for you to know that. Think about it."

I thought about it for some time. The idea of choosing my feelings, of accepting responsibility for them, was a new idea to me. It was not the kind of concept that I digested quickly, but Dr. Perry told me it would not be. I continued to study the idea, to see if I could fully understand it and to see if it had benefit for me.

I stayed with Dr. Perry for a long time. Taken as a whole, my experience with him was moderately productive. Dr. Perry mostly just listened, and often in an aloof kind of way. By the time I saw him in the evening, he had been working with people's problems all day. He was tired, and he often yawned. I often felt he was not really interested in what I was telling him. At times he seemed bored. Maybe I misunderstood him. In any case, I never achieved a great deal of confidence in him.

In addition, he was cool to the idea of religion. My faith in Jesus Christ was becoming more and more important to me, and he was not enthusiastic about it. He was neutral, perhaps, but his lack of enthusiasm struck me as disapproval. I needed more curiosity about what I was going through, and more enthusiasm about methods of fighting back. Maybe I was unrealistic.But about the only answer I was getting out of all this analysis was: "Change the type of person you are." At the same time, I was hearing: "Be yourself." The apparent contradiction mystified me and had a discouraging effect on my hope.

If it was necessary to change the type of person I was, I was willing to try, but I needed some guidelines. Some strategies. How did I go about it? What specific actions should I take? Should I put myself in particular situations? Avoid other situations? I wanted those kinds of answers, and I couldn't get any.

On the one hand, I began to resent Dr. Perry. He was not enthused about our house church, my new faith, or my athletic pursuits. Yet he offered me no other suggestions or ideas. But my positive feelings about Dr. Perry were there, too. For instance, it felt good to pour out my feelings to somebody, and I felt that by seeing him each week, at least I was trying. I was making a fight of it. I was not giving up. Also, I was learning. I was understanding more about myself, my past, and the nature of my anxiety disorder. So I kept going to Dr. Perry. Therapy remained a source of some hope.

The weeks became months and then more months. I kept going to therapy, toughing out one day after another, being active in house church, and running two or three miles a day. I kept playing racquetball, praying, loving my wife and child, and hoping.

I was making some progress. My feelings of terror were abating a little bit. By the month of May, I began to have occasional calm periods during the day. At night, I began to get three hours of sleep, instead of the usual one. When spring came, I got involved in more outdoor activities, and that seemed to help. I was still in the fight of my life, and I knew it, every day. But I was making some progress.

Eight

*T*hen, in June, we took a trip. I didn't know it then, but this trip would have long-range consequences. Judy, Jason, and I went back to Illinois for summer vacation. We went to visit my parents in Monticello.

It turned out to be quite a nostalgic trip for me. This little town was the one I had grown up in, where I finished elementary school. We had moved away in 1955, but here it was, 1974, and my father had been reappointed to the Monticello church. So when we went to visit, we stayed in the very house in which I had grown up.

It was an amazing two weeks. People I had known years before accepted me with a special warmth. They accepted my wife and our son in the same way.

I spent some time visiting with my first grade teacher, a little old lady who was stooped over. She still lived alone on a farm, hauled her own coal, and drove her own car. It had been more than twenty six years since I had been her pupil, yet she remembered me clearly, and we had a nice talk. She said she remembered me as enthusiastic, open, and capable.

I visited my old grade school, where I visualized former teachers and classmates. I sat in the classrooms where I had grown up with those classmates. I went into the cafeteria, where I remembered the music contests I had won for my trumpet solos. I went out into the schoolyard and remembered participating on the softball and basketball teams years before. I remembered being regarded as a good athlete by the coaches, with a good future in athletics. I relived many wonderful memories.

I ran my laps every day on the old track out behind the high school. Some mornings I ran with Willis, an old friend. One hot morning, after finishing our laps, we flopped down together on the grass. The grass was soft and green. Sweat ran freely down my face and neck. I stared off to the right, at the two baseball diamonds. I had played four years of little league baseball on those fields, and so had Willis.

"Do you remember little league?" I asked him.

"Sure," he smiled. "You were on First State Bank and I was on Kapp Chevrolet."

"That's right," I laughed. The sun was warm, the sky was blue, and I felt great. "Willis, I remember the first game you played, you hit one way out by the fence. You got a triple out of it, but you tried to stretch it into a home run, and you got thrown out at the plate."

Now Willis laughed. "I remember, I remember. Man, you've got a good memory. You're going back twenty five years."

We laughed and laughed together. I felt wonderful. That vivid memory filled me with joy and warmth.

Besides Willis's, I renewed many friendships with people I had not seen for years. Everyone seemed to be affirming me. People made it clear that they were genuinely glad to see me. This reception came at a time when I was feeling worthless. It came at a time when I was feeling ashamed and incompetent. It was a wonderful relief to feel worthwhile and so appreciated.

Many days, I took Jason and Judy for long walks. We walked up one street and down another. We stopped for backyard talks with people I remembered from years ago. I seemed to find a memory in every alley—on almost every corner.

For me, it was homecoming. Since I had grown up in a parsonage family, we had done quite a bit of moving around from town to town during my childhood and youth. It had always been difficult for me to answer the question, "What's your home town?" This, however, felt like home. The warmth of this reception caused me to feel like I was home; I had roots. The roots seemed secure and comforting. My "home town" felt warm and reassuring.

I wanted to move there. I wanted to drop everything in the state of New York and move back to my home town. It didn't matter that I had no job in Illinois, or no job prospect. I still wanted to move there. I wanted to live in that warmth and reassurance. I wanted my son to grow up there and be near his grandparents.

I did not tell Judy. I was afraid it was just too crazy. A person didn't just quit a good, secure job, and go to a different place, with no job in sight. So I kept my desire to myself.

We went back to New York. The urge to move back to Illinois dominated my thoughts, but I still did not admit it to Judy. I thought of every reason why it was out of the question. It would be "chickening out." It would be running away from a problem, or trying to. It was irrational. There was no job for me in Illinois. We had good friends in New York, friends that would be difficult to leave.

Still, I couldn't get rid of the desire. I told my therapist about it. Dr. Perry dismissed it: "Your problems won't go away just by changing your setting." I did not have enough assertiveness to challenge him, although I felt like doing so. I was intimidated. So I kept my wish to myself after that; I did not mention it to him again.

In mid-August, I got an invitation from Ron, a friend of mine who taught geography, to take a canoe trip. He wanted to canoe the Allegash in Maine, or the West Branch of the Penobscot River, also in Maine. I told him I would think about it. I had just about dismissed the idea from my mind, when one afternoon, I happened to mention it to Judy.

"Well? Are you going to go with him?" she asked.

"Oh, I doubt it."

"Why? I think you should go. It sounds like fun."

"Oh, I don't really care that much about canoeing," I said.

"Sure you do. You love canoeing. Why don't you go?"

"I just wouldn't feel right, going someplace like that, and leaving you and Jason at home."

"Nonsense. What's the real reason?"

I felt a tightening in my stomach again and tried to dismiss the subject. "I just don't feel like going."

"You're afraid to go," she said suddenly and quietly.

"Me? Afraid of what?"

"Yes, you're afraid." She persisted. She would not let the subject drop. She knew when to be firm with me, so I wouldn't baby myself. She knew when to support and when to push.

I began to tighten up a little more. "Well, I might be a little afraid," I admitted.

"What are you afraid of?"

The tightness inside of me twisted itself into a ball. "O.K.! I am afraid! I'm *afraid!*"

"Of what?"

The tremendous pressure inside turned to anger. "I'm afraid of being somewhere else! I'm afraid to be without control, in a situation that I don't control! I'm afraid of something that's different."

"Calm down."

"I'm afraid! I'm terrified! I'm terrified of the whole world!"

"Try to calm down."

I tried for a while, and finally did calm down, a little bit.

"Ever since your breakdown," said Judy quietly, "you've lost your spontanaeity. You don't do anything on the spur of the moment."

"You're telling me?" I asked. "My whole life is calculated."

"Why?"

"Because I'm terrified of the unknown. I don't trust my emotions to accept what is spontaneous or different. I crave activities that I'm sure of, that I'm used to. Whatever makes me feel in control."

"You can't spend the rest of your life living like that, where will you ever have any fun? What will you enjoy?"

"I don't care about fun, I care about surviving. I do what I have to do to survive." It was the most neurotic thing I had ever said, but I meant it.

"Don't you see, Jim? That's why you *should* go on the canoe trip. You could prove something to yourself. You could show yourself that you can deal with a situation that's out of the ordinary. Maybe you could even enjoy life a little bit instead of fighting with it."

There was no question that her advice made sense. I knew it and had often given myself the same advice. I promised her I would think about it.

For two days, I did think about it. In my mind, I argued one way, then the other. The longer I argued with myself, the more pitiful I felt. I was being ripped apart by a decision that most people were capable of making without a second thought.

I got up in the middle of the night and pounded my right fist into my left palm. "I'm going!" I announced. "I'm going, I'm going, I'm going on that canoe trip."

The next day Ron and I went to the store to buy supplies. We bought everything canned or in tins so we could conserve space by avoiding a cooler. Enough food for ten days had to be carried in just two canoes.

I stood by the Dinty Moore beef stew, terror clutching at me; I saw myself in the wilds of Maine, alone and afraid. I nearly backed out, but Ron got me interested in other supplies.

We started out early the next morning in Ron's car. Ron's son and another teen-aged boy were with us. We had supplies and two tents; we would get the canoes from an outfitter in central Maine.

We drove north throughout the day. Fear clutched my stomach as we went deeper and deeper into the wilderness; the only roads were dirt logging trails, maintained, more or less, by the paper companies. Late that night, when it became obvious that we could not reach the outfitter until the next day, we pulled off and decided to sleep by the edge of the road. We got out our sleeping bags and laid them out in the weeds next to the road.

We did not know it, but we were lying next to a stream. The mosquitoes were deadly. We spent the whole night swatting bugs and not sleeping. I felt a terror filling my stomach, and it was too late to decide not to go on the trip.

The next day about noon, weary and haggard, we reached our destination. Ron arranged with the outfitter to rent the canoes and transport us upriver. With my eyes burning and weariness racking my body, I looked at Ron's car and longed to drive home. I did not want to begin nine days on a lonely river, but it was too late to back out. My fears were intensified by this fact. I was about as miserable as I had ever been during those past eight months. I gave myself a stern pep talk, which had no beneficial effect.

The outfitter loaded the two aluminum canoes onto the top of his Scout and took us deep into the timber, upriver. We started our trip on the West Branch of the Penobscot.

For nine days, the four of us floated our way through the wilderness, using basic maps. We did not see another human being during that period of time.

We floated through that pristine environment, looking at elk, deer, waterfowl, and many square miles of pine forest. I did not enjoy the experience; I was miserable. I was in terror the whole time. I suffered through night after night without sleep, curled into a tight ball. It was the worst ten days of my life, and it filled me with sorrow, because I saw that I couldn't get along without my support system.

One morning Ron said, "You look lousy."

I was embarrassed and irritable. "I'm having trouble sleeping."

"Are you cold at nights?"

"A little," I said, not wanting to discuss the issue.

"You don't seem to be yourself on this trip," he observed.

I did not want to discuss my problem with him. "I'll be O.K.," I said quickly.

On the next to the last day of the trip, late in the afternoon, the river widened into a small lake. The wind was strong, and the water was rough with whitecaps. Suddenly, the boys' canoe tipped over. Ron and I jumped in after them. The four of us were soaking as we pulled the canoe to a nearby island and rescued the overturned supplies.

Finally, we got everything safely onto the shore of an island. The island was sandy and had a few scrubby pine trees. We stripped off all of our clothes and let the sun and wind dry us. It felt strange to be standing naked out of doors, but there were no people nearby, nor were there likely to be.

"You're getting skinny," said Ron.

"I know," I said. I was about 145 pounds now.

Later, we got on our dry clothes, built a fire, and cooked some canned stew. Then we heated some water, and Ron and I fixed coffee. "Look what I found in the crook of this tree," said Ron.

He was holding an old cigar, half-smoked. "Look what the natives left behind."

We sat on the warm beach, watching the sunset. We smoked the old, stale cigar, passing it back and forth. We enjoyed the coffee. I felt a certain calm settle over me. I felt peaceful for a while, and that was encouraging. It was an odd set of ingredients that generated this peacefulness, but nevertheless that's what happened.

When the trip was over I was exhausted and shaken. And grateful to be home. I hugged Judy and Jason joyfully.

I did not enjoy the trip and I did not have "fun." It was thus clear to me that I had now adopted a lifestyle that I could only think to call a "defense lifestyle." The weapons that I had developed to fight against my disorder were now my whole life. I was consciously structuring every day, right to the hour, if possible, with predictably absorbing activities.

Every day had to be programmed to include running, teaching, sports, playing with Jason, and all the rest. I made certain that no day had any free time in it, or any time I had to spend alone. My support system was now my whole life. I couldn't stand the threat of any loose time, or anything spontaneous. Time that was not structured was very threatening. Anything that caused me to rearrange my schedule was equally threatening. It was very disheartening to see the kind of prison I had built for myself. Yet I felt that I had to survive, and I knew no other way of doing it. I was doing what I had to do.

The fall semester started. I kept toughing it out, one day at a time. I spent much time in prayer and meditation. I kept going to Dr. Perry for therapy.

In November, I had another breakdown.

For two days and nights, wave after wave of acute anxiety racked me. I was weeping and trembling and barely able to function—to have a conversation, to hold a class. I went out into the fields one cold, windy November night and cried and cried.

I felt defeated. All I had done, all my work and effort, were now as nothing. I saw myself as miserable and useless.

The next night was my night to see Dr. Perry. I told him of this new breakdown, of the terror, of the dislocation. "Everything I've done is worthless," I said. "I haven't found the answer."

"Everything you have done is not worthless," he disagreed firmly. "There is simply more to do, and more to understand."

"How can I do more? I'm working day and night to get better."

"You're working too hard. You need to try working less."

Then I got mad. "You sit where I'm sitting and try to work less!" I started yelling at him, "You let it clutch at your guts for a while and see if you take it easy! You go through it for a while and see how you handle it!"

Dr. Perry was a little shocked, but he was supportive. "I guess I deserved that," he said quietly. "It is easy to judge when we are not the one who is suffering. I'm glad you got mad, though; you ought to do that more often."

"I'm not really mad at you," I said. "I'm mad at the curse."

"I know you're not mad at me," he said. "So don't be afraid to yell at me."

"O.K., O.K.," I said, still angry.

"Don't feel like everything you've done is for nothing," he continued. "It may not be enough, but it doesn't count for nothing."

Much discouraged, I went home. Late that night, I gushed it all out to Judy. I wept bitterly and said I wanted to call my mother.

"Then go ahead," she said. So I called, and tried to tell my mother what was happening. "My life may be over," I said desperately. "I think that I might be cracking up." But then I was sobbing too much to continue talking.

My mother was terribly concerned, and the next day she flew to New York to spend some time with us. We had supper together and afterward I told her and Judy I wanted to move to Illinois. I wanted to move "home." I told them that everywhere I went in our New York environment I made an association with fear and despair. I wanted to make a new start in Illinois.

"Your problems won't go away just by moving," said my mother.

"I know, I know. I still want to move."

"When would we go?" asked Judy.

"I'm not exactly sure," I said. "How about next June? When the school year is over."

Judy nodded, trying to absorb all of this. She was afraid and disappointed.

Then I told her, "I've wanted to tell you this, but I've been afraid to; it sounds so crazy."

"What would we do in Illinois?" she asked.

"I'm not sure. I could try to get a job teaching. But I'd rather try to find some religious vocation. I want to serve Jesus Christ."

"What kind of religious vocation?"

"I'm not sure. I'd have to check it out. I'd just like to be involved in religious work if I can. The Lord is very important to me. I'd like to have my faith and my work come together."

"But wouldn't you have to go to a seminary first?"

"Well, I don't think I want to be a minister. There are other kinds of Christian work. Maybe it could be youth work, as a lay staff member in a large church. Maybe campus foundation work, or work in a campus religious organization. Maybe religious education."

"I never thought of those things," she said.

"Look, I would just like some Christian involvement in my work, if there is any way. My faith is that important to me."

Then my mother said, "Well, if you settled in Champaign-Urbana, you would probably find some opportunities at the University of Illinois. There are many campus foundations there."

I brightened. "That's a good idea."

"There's also a new junior college there," she added.

That night, in bed, Judy said to me, "I can't sleep."

"Me neither. Are you thinking about Illinois?"

"Yes, I am. It will be awfully hard to leave our friends."

"I know it will," I said. I knew how right she was. I thought immediately of Dick Dutton and how terribly I would miss him if we moved.

We sat on the edge of the bed and looked out the bedroom window. The moonlight was bright on the frosty ground. I held her hand. Hearing Judy mention the pain of leaving friends, I was plunged into a pit of second-guessing.

Inside, I felt a terrible dilemma. I feared I couldn't survive if we stayed in New York, yet what right did I have to utterly disrupt Judy's life? Or Jason's? Judy's identity was here, in New York. She had meaningful friendships here, and many activities that gratified her. She was extremely close to the members of our house church family. She worked as a phone volunteer for county mental health, listening and referring. She volunteered her time to help pattern children who were mentally retarded. She was very active in a community group that worked with abusive parents and encouraged creative child-rearing. She was a caring Christian, much gratified in those helping activities of community service. Much of who she was was here, in those important connections.

Why should she drop all this to follow her neurotic husband on what could turn out to be a wild goose chase? Why should she sacrifice all this on the altar of my madness? My stomach seized in panic as I followed this train of thought.

Furthermore, what if nothing changed in Illinois? What if my disorder continued on the same acute level? What then? Then I would have to deal with it all without money and without the established support system I had here in New York. And even further, if that happened, how did I expect to be able to serve God? What made me think I could be of any use to the Lord, when I couldn't do much more than survive from day to day?

I didn't know what to do. I did not have the vaguest notion of what was a wise or an unwise decision. I buried my face in my hands, and Judy put her arm around me.

"I love our friends in house church," Judy said. "I'm so close to them."

"I know," I said, feeling utterly wretched. I could not bring myself to ask her to leave New York. It was not fair.

Then she said, "But I would like Jason to live nearer to my folks and to your folks."

"It isn't fair," I said. "I have no right to ask you."

"I'm not sure fair has anything to do with it," she said. "There isn't anything fair about all of this we've been going through."

"I can't disrupt your whole life," I said. "I can't make you give up everything."

For a few moments we sat in silence.

Then Judy said, "I'll never be happy if you are miserable. Let's do what it takes to get you well."

"There's no guarantee starting over in Illinois will help," I said. "It might be phony. Dr. Perry is suspicious of the whole idea. There's no guarantee."

"I know that," Judy said. "But maybe it's worth a try. We've tried everything else, haven't we?"

"Everything I can think of."

"Then let's try it."

I put my arms around her and said, "I feel a terrible guilt. I shouldn't do this to you."

We held each other for some time. I felt tears stinging my eyes. She was sticking by me even through this, and I didn't feel deserving.

Finally, Judy said quietly, "We have to try it."

At breakfast the next morning we talked with excitement about our decision. My mother was in high spirits, hearing about the decision. The wisest course seemed to be to try and settle in Champaign-Urbana. The resources of a Big Ten University were considerable, and I felt optimistic. Since I had grown up in that part of the state, I was familiar with the community.

Thus, we had made a huge decision. It was both frightening and exhilarating. Frightening for all the obvious problems, and exhilarating in the fact that a major decision had been made.

After this second breakdown, I felt as though I was starting all over, as if I had it all to do over again. I began with determination, trying to take one day at a time. I still did not have the answers I wanted; I still had the uneasy feeling that there were constructive things I could be doing for myself, if only I knew just what they were.

Without patience, I took my way through the next weeks. It was early December, but I was committed to finishing the school year at my college. That stretched my commitment through the following month of May. It would be a long six months and I knew it, but I was determined to stick it out.

I began each day with prayer. My time in prayer was no longer exclusively desperate. Much of the time, I went to God in hope. My pain had not been removed, yet I did not despair of God's love, nor did I lose faith.

I still prayed for help and for strength to carry on. And I prayed for increased understanding of myself, that I might be able to overcome my disorder. I often sat outside on a stump on cold evenings, beneath the stars. If there was enough moonlight, I pulled out my trusty New Testament that my father had given me years before. The words of Jesus lifted me up: "I am the bread of life; he who comes to me shall not hunger, and he who believes in me shall never thirst. . . . If any one thirst, let him come to me and drink. He who believes in me, as the Scripture has said, Out of his heart shall flow rivers of living water. . . . I am the light of the world; he who follows me will not walk in darkness, but will have the light of life"(John 6:35; 7:37; 8:12 RSV).

At those moments I often felt the presence of Christ as a trusted and valued friend. I looked forward to spending time with Him, in His presence.

I also began to pray for others regularly, to ask for sensitivity that I might be mindful of the needs of others. I prayed for members of our house church family, particularly Karen, who was still suffering so deeply with her blindness. Because of my own acute hurt, I tried to remember in my prayers others who were hurting.

In late December, we spent our Christmas vacation in Illinois. I spent much of my time making some contacts in the Champaign-Urbana community that might help me in the job hunt that would soon be coming. I spent time on the campus of the University of Illinois. I familiarized myself with the religious foundations on campus, where they were, and what kind of staffing they had.

I shared our decision to move to Illinois with several old friends from Monticello. They were pleased to hear it and promised to keep their eyes open for likely job possibilities.

I put in an application at Parkland Community College in Champaign. I had much experience at the community college level. I went and talked with the sports editor of the Champaign *News-Gazette*. I had experience in journalism, and I thought newspaper work might be an opportunity for me.

"Why do you want to leave teaching?" he asked.

"We want to move back to this part of Illinois," I said. "I feel that it's home."

"How much money are you making in New York?" he asked.

"About twenty thousand dollars," I answered.

"Then I'd stay right there, if I were you. You can't begin to make that kind of money writing for a newspaper—certainly not this newspaper."

I laughed. "It's not the money," I said. "I want to be here. I don't mind making less money."

He shook his head, mystified. I had to laugh again. Finally, he said, "Well, I'll sure help you out if something comes up, but I still say, stay where you are."

It was my first exposure to disbelief concerning my decision. I was to encounter the same response again and again. Naturally, I didn't feel inclined to outline my mental history for him, but I assured him I really was going to resign from my job and relocate in Illinois. He promised to let me know if anything opened up.

During the remainder of that holiday period, I continued to check out possible leads. My first priority was Christian work, but I knew that I might not get what I wanted, at least not right away. So I followed any lead that seemed promising, secular or religious. It was fun; I met a lot of interesting people, and I was not yet under pressure to get results.

Nine

We drove back to New York.

I was so terribly impatient to move to Illinois that I was often tempted simply to quit my job and go right away. But I didn't do it. Deciding to go was enough. I could finish the second semester first. But during that entire semester, the conflict tore at me—my commitment to finish the semester, versus wanting to return to Illinois immediately.

On a wintry March morning, I told the academic dean of my decision to resign and move to Illinois. He took off his glasses and stared at me across his desk. "You're kidding," he said.

"No," I said, "I'm not kidding. I've made a decision."

"What's the matter? Is something the matter?"

"Oh, one or two things, but they're personal; there's no complaint with the college."

"Are you sure about this, Jim?"

I felt a bit guilty, because I liked him. "I'm sure. The decision is made."

"What will you do in Illinois; will you be teaching?"

"I may be; it remains to be seen."

He put his glasses back on. "I suppose it's no use to try to talk you out of it?"

"No. I've made up my mind," I said firmly but politely.

"We will miss you," he said.

"I'll miss you, too," I said. "I do have a favor to ask."

"Anything."

"I'd like you to write a letter of recommendation for me, to go with my credentials."

"I'll be glad to." He stood up, and we shook hands. He held my right hand in both of his hands. "We will miss you," he repeated. "You are a good teacher."

"Thank you."

Leaving his office, I went back upstairs to my own office and closed the door. I typed a brief letter of resignation to the president, and signed it. I made a couple of copies, kept one, put one in the president's mailbox, and one in the dean's mailbox. I stood for several moments and looked at the letters resting in the mailboxes. This was a big moment; this act made the decision official. I felt elated and scared. I wished I had a crystal ball; what did life hold for me and my family during the next months and years?

I told many close friends of our decision to move. I did not tell them the whole reason why, just that I wanted to be in Illinois, that I wanted to be in some kind of Christian vocation, and that Judy and I wanted our son to live nearer his grandparents. I did not tell them of the emotional disorder I was going through or of my struggle to overcome it.

I was not happy with this situation. I wanted to tell my friends the whole truth; I had been working hard to eliminate untruths from my life and a half-truth was about like a lie, I felt. I was not afraid to reveal my struggle—by now, I had gotten rid of most of the shame connected with it. But I simply did not have enough energy to explain it all to everyone.

As the semester wore on, I began making progress

again. I began experiencing periods of calm. I began to get more sleep. I continued to use all of my weapons, from running to prayer.

One pleasant spring night in April, I was at a prayer meeting with seminarians at the Catholic seminary near our campus. Father Dale, who was on the faculty at our college, was advisor to the prayer group and he had invited me to come, which I often did.

On this particular night, after prayers, the two of us walked together in the courtyard, surrounded by the stone Gothic residence halls of the seminary. We had passed a few minutes in small talk when suddenly he turned to me and said, "I've got something I need to talk with somebody about. I need a confessor," he smiled.

I was a little startled. I perceived Father Dale as a person who had his act together, spiritually, mentally, and every other way. "What can I do for you?" I asked.

"Do you remember in prayers how I asked the Lord to help those who have difficult decisions to make?"

"Yes, I do," I said.

"Come upstairs with me," he said.

We went upstairs in one of the residences to his two rooms. One was a sitting room, one a bedroom. He swung open two windows, old leaded ones with crank handles. A fresh breeze came in. We sat down in easy chairs.

"A priest has nobody to talk to most of the time," he began. "Everybody wants us to listen to his problems, but what about our problems?"

I nodded. I could understand.

"I've gotten to know you at the prayer meetings," he said. "I like you and I trust you; I think I can talk with you."

I was very curious, but not uncomfortable. I was used to intimate sharing. He looked at me, leaned back in his chair, and folded his hands behind his head. Father Dale was handsome and athletic, with hair that was cut short and prematurely gray; he was in his middle thirties. It took him a long time to find the words he wanted.

Finally he said, "I've been having a very difficult problem I can't understand. It's something I pray about every day."

I didn't quite know what to say, as I didn't really know Father Dale intimately. "I'll listen the best I can," I said.

He looked at me very seriously and said quietly, "Last year, I had a mental breakdown."

I was stunned. I sat up very straight, hungry for more information. "Go on," I urged. "Go on, tell me more."

"I don't know what else to call it," he said. "I just woke up every day, terrorized. I was shaking with fear, and there was no cause. It went on for weeks and weeks."

I looked at him and noticed that he was much thinner than he had been a year ago.

"How long did this go on?" I asked.

"Weeks. Months. I thought I was cracking up, you know, a goner. I would be eating breakfast with the seminary guys here at the cafeteria and I was just tied in a knot."

"Dale!" I said loudly. "I've been going through exactly the same thing, ever since last January, fifteen months ago!"

"You have?"

"Yes!" I laughed. "Exactly the same. Week after week, month after month, I didn't know if I'd make it through the day."

He seemed astonished. "This is incredible! Did you feel constant terror, with no cause for it?"

"Exactly!" I declared. "Exactly the same." We doubled up with laughter and slapped each other on the back. For the next three hours we compared notes about what we had felt, what had helped, what had not helped. We were both in a state of joy to find another human being who had suffered through the same thing. I told him I had always perceived him as a person who was on top of life, and he said he had always had the same perception of me.

That night fortified me. I did not feel like quite such a freak; I was not the only one. Father Dale and I were intimate friends after that, spending many evenings together in searching, sharing conversations. It was much more helpful than any formal therapy, because it was two fellow sufferers supporting each other. He was a deeply committed Christian, and so was I. We shared our faith, and we prayed for each other often. We were providing each other with two vital elements: *careful listening,* and *Christian love.* There is no more important combination of elements for one in the pain of emotional dislocation. My close relationship to Father Dale lifted me up many times throughout that troubled spring.

During that time I wrote a number of letters of inquiry, exploring the job possibilities in Champaign-Urbana. Though I applied for some teaching positions, none was available—a fact that did not surprise me. This was 1975, and I was a teacher in the humanities. There was a large oversupply of teachers, particularly in my field, but I was not discouraged; I was excited to be going home.

The end of May came. The last final exam was marked, the last grade card turned in. The final reports were completed.

The day before we left was Sunday; we had an emotional leave-taking from our house church family. We formed a circle and held hands; we sang "One in the Spirit," with tears stinging our eyes.

Judy and I held Dick Dutton and his family for a long time. "Never give up," Dick said to me. "I'll have you in my prayers."

I hated to leave him. No person had done more to help

me or had shown me more clearly the nature of Christian love. Judy felt precisely the same.

That evening, I went to the seminary and said good-bye to Father Dale. We, too, had tears in our eyes as we hugged one another a final time.

The following day, we loaded all of our belongings into a sixteen-foot U-Haul truck. We hooked up our Volkswagen to the back of the truck and headed west. As we drove along the highway, my feelings were ambivalent: I knew precisely what I was leaving behind, but what lay ahead? Was this a right decision, or merely a swap-out of problems? I tried not to think such thoughts.

Twenty miles down the road, our car began riding unevenly. I stopped to check it. The bumper hook-up was pulling the car bumper out of shape. Soon, the car bumper probably would have broken loose from tow. Thus, Judy had to drive the car the rest of the 980 miles while I drove the truck. Jason took turns riding with each of us. Driving two vehicles made travel more difficult, but we did manage to stay together.

We arrived in Illinois on the first of June. We stored all of our belongings in my parents' garage, and for the time being we moved in with them.

Ten

*F*or several days we relaxed in the community of Monticello. I took walks with Judy and Jason, and talked over old times with many friends. I joined a men's church softball team and had fun playing ball.

After those few days, however, I began serious job-hunting. I had my future to take care of, and the future of my family. Each morning, I drove the twenty miles to Champaign-Urbana and the University of Illinois campus. I began visiting the religious foundations on campus. I visited the Newman Center, the Wesley Foundation, the Lutheran Student Center, and many others. In each case I talked with the director of the foundation to determine what staffing it had and what I might be qualified for. Most people were helpful. If they had nothing available, they agreed to listen to the grapevine for me, and they sometimes had some helpful suggestions.

It became clear that the nation's sluggish economy was being felt by campus religious foundations; in most cases they were being forced by funding realities to cut back, not expand, their programming operations. My background and education qualified me for several positions of the kind that were part of religious foundations, but openings were very rare. Still, I kept checking, as each contact I made tended to lead to one or two others.

One morning I spoke to the director of the McKinley Foundation, which was the Presbyterian student center on campus. I told him of my background, our decision to move back to Illinois, and what type of situation I wanted to find.

"I respect what you've done then," he said. "It sounds like a decision that took some courage."

"Don't make it more courageous than it is," I said quickly. "A big part of my reason for coming back to Illinois was to find security."

"Still, it takes a certain courage to decide what you value and then to make a commitment to it."

I didn't disagree anymore. I thought I had made my feelings clear, and I was trying to learn not to discredit myself at every turn.

The director was a lean man in his forties, with dark-rimmed glasses. He wore a tweed sports jacket with leather patches on the elbows, and he smoked a pipe continuously. He went on talking. "I've heard of a job you might be interested in. The Campus YWCA has an opening for a director of activities for senior citizens. Have you ever worked with the elderly?"

"Not really."

"Would you object to working with them?"

"No, of course not."

"I was talking with the YWCA director just this morning," he continued. "That's when she told me about the position. It doesn't pay much, and it isn't very exciting, I don't imagine. Still, senior citizens are often lonely people who need support. The need is there. It might be gratifying work. I could call Barbara up right now, if you'd like."

I was interested. "Sure," I said. "I would appreciate it."

He used the phone on his desk and called. "Hello, Barbara? I have a young man with a strong education background here in my office. He's interested in starting a second career. I told him about the opening you have."

He was silent for a few moments, listening.

"O.K., listen, I want to tell you that he's a man and he's white. Are you in a position to hire any white males?"

The answer came back: regrettably, no.

He hung up the phone and turned to me. "Affirmative action."

I nodded my head, not knowing what to say.

He went on: "Most everybody wants to hire blacks or women right now. That's where consciousness is at. I know that doesn't help you very much."

"No," I said.

"I tell you what. I'll keep my eyes and ears open. Make sure I've got your telephone number and your name. And don't get too discouraged; something will turn up."

We shook hands, and I left. I had been experiencing a lot of firsts lately. So far as I knew, this was the first time I had ever been the target of racial or sexual discrimination.

As I left the building, I happened to look back. Over the entrance to the McKinley Foundation was a large banner with these words: "If God be for us, who can be against us?" I stood for some time looking at the sign. Inside, I felt a surge of encouragement. I knew that in the days and weeks to come I would need to remember that banner. Whatever developed, I was not alone, and with God's help, sooner or later I would find what I needed.

After several weeks of driving back and forth to Champaign-Urbana, I realized that it was necessary for us to find a home in that community. If that was where the opportunities were most likely to occur, then we ought to live there. I talked it over with Judy, and she agreed: it was time to move to Champaign-Urbana.

After a few days of hunting, we located a small house for rent in southwest Champaign. It was exactly what we wanted, and the rent was modest. But we had to convince the landlord that he should rent to an unemployed family. I explained to him that I had a very stable employment record, and that I had college and advanced degrees. I told him I was a good worker. I also told him I planned to be choosy: I would not accept just any job. He was a local businessman and reluctant to give in, but he finally did.

We loaded everything into another U-Haul truck and moved into the small house. So we now had a house, but no job and no good lead. I was about to find out that starting over is tough. My job hunt would continue to be difficult for two reasons. First, I intended to be picky. I wanted a Christian vocation if I could find it, and if not, then some other kind of people-helping work. Second, I would not take any eight-to-five job, or any job that required me to be in an office for regular hours. These two preconditions eliminated hundreds of jobs. For me, the field was very narrow.

My refusal to consider any eight-to-five job, of course, was a direct result of my emotional disorder. My anxiety attacks were often so severe that I literally could not sit still. I had to have a physical outlet when I needed it. This meant that I had to have the freedom to walk out, run laps, play racquetball, or do something to work through the tension. Being trapped in an office terrified me, as I would be without that essential freedom.

In addition, I had been a college teacher for ten years. I had always had a great deal of freedom in deciding what my working hours would be. It was a freedom and independence that I was not willing to forfeit. I knew what I could handle and what I could not. It did mean, though, that my job opportunities would be sharply limited.

I went out each day, following leads, looking for work. I applied for any position that looked like it might satisfy. I remember going to interview for a position as an editor with a local publisher. The woman who was doing the hiring showed me into her office. She was very businesslike and well dressed.

"Good morning, Mr. Bennett. I have been looking over your credentials here. You have a strong background in literature and education, which is essentially what we are looking for." She took off her glasses and looked at me, across her desk.

"Before we start interviewing," I said, "I need to ask you a question. Is this an eight-to-five job?"

"Well, yes, actually, it is," she said.

"People who work here come to the office and stay in the office throughout the work day?"

"Yes. Why?"

"Then I wouldn't be interested," I said quietly. "I don't want a job that confines me to an office."

She blinked.

I went on. "Please don't take it personally, I'm just trying to save us both a lot of time."

I got up, we shook hands, and I left. I had that same conversation, or one very similar, in a number of different offices, on a number of different occasions.

There were several interesting leads that I followed. I put in applications at several of the religious foundations on campus, even though there were no current openings. I applied for a job as an editor for the medical school at the University. It was an attractive job, but I ran into the "white male" problem again, and then too, I was in competition against a number of highly-qualified people.

For that matter, the university community was bursting with educated, capable people. Most of those people were forced to take jobs that did not challenge them or fulfill their capabilities. The teacher market was so oversupplied with trained people that schools could hire qualified teachers as teachers' aides. In education, that situation still exists.

I investigated the academic positions at the University Athletic Association. The A.A. had positions for tutors who could help and counsel athletes on athletic scholarship. I had lots of experience teaching remedial English and lots of knowledge about athletics. But nothing opened up.

My search continued in this fashion for several weeks. I prayed every morning and every night for God's help. The first of September came, and we still had no income. We were paying rent and bills out of our savings, which were dwindling fast. We were about to find out what poverty was like.

Judy had decided she would like to work too, preferably part-time. She got the first job. She went to work half-time in a small gift shop on campus. She earned minimum wage, about $2.30 per hour.

Her job lasted two weeks, and then she got laid off because the gift shop was not doing any business.

Because I was still not having any luck at all, I signed up with Manpower, Incorporated, temporary services. This development was not a happy one. It was necessary for me to go to the Manpower office early in the morning and wait there for employers to call. It was a dirty office with a hopeless atmosphere. There was a vinyl counter behind which were three secretaries who answered telephones, gave out job assignments, and did a great deal of filing. The floor was dirty green tile with dozens of crushed cigarette butts. There were molded plastic chairs to sit on, many of them cracked. The room itself was thick with cigarette haze and the ceiling tiles were yellowed.

The applicants were young and old, black and white, thick and thin. Some of them had no teeth and had not shaved. They looked like they had stepped out of a soup line during the depression. Some of the men played cards, others read newspapers, and still others smoked cigarettes and gazed vacantly out the window. The room was hot, without a fan or air-conditioner.

I learned from conversations that sometimes you could wait all day and not get a job, whereas on other days, you might get a job the moment you walked into the office. I spent my first day there, miserable and lonely. Less than four months previous, I had taken home a paycheck of more than five hundred dollars every two weeks.

In the afternoon, I struck up a conversation with a man who had a master's degree in psychology. He was an interesting man; he liked as much free time in his life as possible. Manpower's system was ideal for him, because his financial needs were small, and he didn't like working more than a couple of days a week.

The next day, I forced myself to go back to the Manpower office. It was wretched, but I couldn't think of anything better to try. That morning, I got a job assignment immediately. Along with three other men, I drove out to a large grain elevator west of town. We spent the day shoveling corn into bins. It was hard work, and hot, but I was glad to be doing something. The job lasted two more days. After a couple more days of idle waiting, I was assigned to the Champaign Park District, mowing grass in the city parks. This, too, was hard work, but it was out of doors, and pleasant to be working in fresh air. That job lasted four days and I got a check from Manpower for $112 for a total of seven days of work.

We had been without income for so long that the paycheck seemed like a lot of money. We went out and celebrated. Our celebration was double cheeseburgers and chocolate milk shakes at a local hamburger joint. It doesn't sound like much, but we were pretty excited about our "success."

While I was on those temporary jobs, Judy was working in the gift shop. That meant we had to find a place to care for Jason. We had no friends to turn to, so we found a group baby sitter. It turned out to be a negative place for Jason. All the children did was watch television. It was not at all stimulating for Jason, who was now two and a half years old and much advanced for his age in social and verbal skills.

Each morning as we left the house, Jason turned to me and said, "I don't have to go to the baby sitter's today, do I?"

"I think we better," Judy and I said.

And then he began to cry.

Judy tried to console him. "Maybe it'll be fun with the other children today." I felt ripped by guilt. It was because of me that we were here, in this community, without prospects. Why should our little guy suffer this disorientation and confusion? It was because of me that Jason had to be cared for in a negative environment.

The next day, I drove to the Wesley Foundation at the University campus; I knew there was a progressive nursery school housed in the Foundation. I walked into one of the classrooms where the teacher, an attractive young woman, was straightening up.

I introduced myself and got quickly to the point: "My wife and I have a little guy who needs to be in a nursery school. Can you take him?"

She was a little taken aback. "How old is he?"

"Two and a half."

"We usually don't take them until they're three."

"Can you make an exception?" I went on, "He's very advanced for his age."

"Is he toilet trained?"

"Yes."

"Well, I do have one opening in the class. I'll have to speak to the director, but I'm willing to give him a try."

"Great," I said. "I'll bring him tomorrow."

"Make it the next day," she said, laughing. "I have to talk to the director first. Are you always this way?" she asked me.

I laughed. "What way?"

"So . . . so persistent?"

I had to think about it for a moment. "Yes, I guess I am, when I know what the answer is."

We shook hands, and I left. I thought about what she had said as I drove home. Because of my mental disorder, I was much more assertive than I had ever been before; I was willing to present my case with less fear. When I saw a clear course of action, I was now quick to make a decision and follow through on it.

At home, I told Judy the good news. "Jason starts nursery school at the Wesley Foundation on Thursday."

"How?" said Judy. "How did you arrange it?"

I told her of my conversation with the teacher at nursery school.

"Why, that's wonderful!" she said. "That's supposed to be a wonderful school."

"That's what he needs," I said.

"How will we afford it?" Judy asked suddenly.

I felt a twinge of panic, but chose to ignore it. "Some way," I said. "Somehow we'll find a way."

Jason was immediately at home in this new setting and very happy to be in it. It was a real school setting, with challenging learning opportunities. The teachers were creative and enthusiastic. Jason's new-found joy was a real uplift to Judy and me.

But my feelings were constantly flip-flopping during this period. I was up, and then I was down. I was hopeful, and then pessimistic. My anxiety level was often very high. I was having serious misgivings. Had I made a huge mistake? Had I run from a problem into a miserable, dead-end situation? Had I dragged my wife and child into a mess just because I couldn't deal with life? Had I dragged their lives down, too?

The anxiety attacks continued, and their severity persisted. I was very scared. Starting over was a trauma. I didn't know if I could get through it. I didn't trust myself or my feelings—I feared that my feelings would jump out of control again. I remembered that Dr. Perry had told me that changing my environment would not change my emotions. I spent a number of sleepless nights and jittery days. I was afraid of cracking.

Then I got a call from a friend of mine, a United Methodist minister named Dale Scott. He was on the staff of the Wesley Foundation. He said he had a line on a job that I might be interested in. The job was with the Champaign County Head Start program.

Head Start is a federally-funded program of preschool education and enrichment for children from economically and culturally disadvantaged homes. Head Start needed a "bus manager." The job called for some bus driving, but mostly I would be supervising drivers and designing efficient bus routes.

I went to interview for the job. The Head Start offices consisted of two modest rooms on the third floor of the Wesley Foundation. Jason's nursery school was on the first floor; it seemed odd, the way I kept interacting with this building one way or another.

The Head Start offices were messy and seemed chaotic. Both rooms were overcrowded with desks, filing cabinets, and people. There was a high noise level, and there were papers, folders, and books piled everywhere. Most of the employees were black; the director, Mr. White, was a black man in his forties. His hair was streaked with gray. We introduced ourselves to one another, and then he took me to his desk in the corner. We tried to talk for a few moments, but there was too much noise, so we went out and stood in the hall.

He described the position briefly. "Our buses are always late, and our routes are inefficient. We need to have them organized, and we need to have them work on schedule."

"What happened to the last supervisor?" I asked.

"We fired him. He couldn't work with black people. He couldn't relate. Can you work with black people?"

"I've always been able to work with the black people I've known," I said. "I guess I don't have a whole lot of experience."

"Tell me about your background," he said.

I told him about my teaching experience, my education, our decision to move to Illinois, and my frustration over not finding the type of work I wanted.

"You're overqualified," he said quickly. "That's your problem."

"Explain that to me," I said. "I've been hearing it a lot lately."

He took off his glasses and massaged his eyes. He looked very tired. I imagined that directing a Head Start program was very difficult. "You have too much education," he said. "People want to hire people who are starting out, working their way up. You've already been up. I know lots of overqualified people. People are afraid that if they hire you, you will hear of something more stimulating and leave, to take the better opportunity. If I hired you, that's what I would worry about."

That was blunt enough. I shrugged. "I guess it's possible," I said quietly.

"Of course, it's possible. You'd be a fool not to keep your eyes open for something more challenging. Have you ever driven a bus before?"

"No," I said.

"Do you know the streets of Champaign-Urbana?"

"No," I had to admit.

He put on his glasses and looked at me. "The job's yours if you want it, " he said. "You can start tomorrow."

I was stunned. I thought we had just determined that I wasn't really suited for the job, yet he was offering it to me.

He laughed at my confusion. "Dale Scott has vouched for you. He says you're resourceful and intelligent. The job's yours if you want it."

We talked some more about the particular responsibilities of the job. It was not really what I was looking for, and the pay was very low, only three dollars an hour. But I took it right away.

I took it because I needed a job of *some* kind. I took it because I liked helping people who needed help. I also took it because, to a large degree, it allowed me the freedom to set my own work hours.

On the way out of the building after my interview, I met the man who had just been fired from the position I was taking. He had come to get his last paycheck. He told me who he was. He had a crew cut and nicks in his scalp. "You the new bus supervisor?"

I said that I was.

"Let me tell you something," he said. "Your headaches are just beginning."

I didn't say anything.

He went on, "You try and work with the niggers, and you'll know what I mean." He turned abruptly and walked out the door, into the parking lot. I felt an apprehensive lump forming in my stomach as I watched him go. With the lump still clogging my insides an hour later at home, I told Judy about my new job.

I had no sooner told her than she began to cry. She sobbed and sobbed. With an ache in my heart, I sat down next to her on the couch and put my arm around her. These were tears of relief mostly, as she explained to me when she was able. "I was afraid we would never get anything," she said. "Sometimes I get so discouraged; I can't help it."

"You don't have to help it," I said. I understood the discouragement.

"I've been afraid," she went on. "I've felt helpless."

I realized then, sharply, how difficult this whole ordeal was for her. I had been so distracted by *my* problems, I had been tending to overlook Judy's problems. I put my arms around her. She had sacrificed so much to follow me here and stick by me; in the days to come, I would make a greater effort to remember that I was not the *only* one with problems. I was not the only one in need of support.

We sat together for some time, there on the couch. After we felt composed, we got Jason and went for cheeseburgers and milkshakes again, in celebration of my new job.

The first thing I had to do at Head Start was get a class C driver's license. That was easy enough. I practiced driving the bus for a couple of days in university parking lots, and then I took my road test. I passed and began driving one of the evening bus routes.

The second thing I had to do was more difficult. I had to organize efficient bus routes in a community where I was pretty much unfamiliar with the streets. But I did have a brain, and I could read street maps. I studied the maps in the evening and marked out some alternate possibilities. Then during the day, I drove each route and timed it. Finally, I combined some of the features of each route and got what I wanted.

By the end of a week, the buses were on time and the children were getting to the Head Start centers on time. They were also getting home on time. Mr. White was pleased. He grinned from ear to ear and said he had been waiting for over a year for the buses to run on time.

There were three drivers at Head Start, all young black men. It appeared they resented having a white supervisor, yet we never discussed it. I gave each of them a color-coded mini-map of his route, with stops and times of stops. They followed the maps well, and the punctual bus routes were the result.

I was scared a good deal of the time, stemming from my anxieties and from the fact the job was something very different from my previous work experiences. I remembered what the previous supervisor had said about working with "niggers." I treated the drivers politely and tried to explain directions clearly, but I did not try to become their friend.

My life of prayer was more important to me now than ever. Each morning I arrived at the Foundation building at 6:30. At that time, no one else was in the building. I had to let myself in with a key. Before going upstairs to the Head Start office, I always went first to the west wing, to the large church sanctuary where I spent several minutes at the altar, on my knees in prayer. The sanctuary was vast and quiet, with the sweet smell of waxed wooden pews. I fixed my eyes on the huge silver cross that hung behind the altar, and I prayed for God to walk with me throughout the day.

There was a denominational book of worship in the sanctuary, which I often used for my private worship. Many of the prayers I prayed again and again, but there soon was one litany that became my favorite, entitled simply "A Recollection of Jesus":

Let us remember Jesus:

> Who, though he was rich, yet for our sakes became poor and dwelt among us . . .
>
> Who was mighty in deed, healing the sick and the disordered, using for others the powers he would not invoke for himself . . .
>
> Who through all disappointment never lost heart . . .
>
> Who disregarded his own comfort and convenience, and thought first of others' needs, and, though he suffered long, was always kind . . .
>
> O Christ, our only Savior, so come to dwell in us that we may go forth with the light of thy hope in our eyes, and with thy faith and love in our hearts. Amen.

Many times I was lifted up by this litany. This love of Jesus was for *me*, not just for others, no matter how incompetent I might feel at times.

"If I can't be normal," I often prayed, "if I must continue to carry an emotional disorder around with me, please let me never feel alone." I trusted the Lord to go with me, whatever I might go through emotionally.

Each evening before I left the building, I went again to the sanctuary for more prayer. I often read from the book of worship or from hymns in the hymnal. At home in the evenings, I read various passages of Scripture, and I prayed for God to walk with me and support me.

One evening as I was praying in the sanctuary, a young woman in blue jeans and a trench coat came rapidly down the center aisle. She was obviously a university student, for she clutched several textbooks to her chest.

I was sitting in the front pew. I doubt that she saw me; she went directly to the altar and fell to her knees, spilling her books loudly onto the floor. She began to sob. My heart went out to her, for even though I had no idea who she was, I knew a great deal about private suffering. I felt very sad inside, listening to her sobs and looking at her shoulders heave up and down. I felt an empathy for her.

Feeling a little embarrassed and uncertain, I went to where she stood and put my arm around her. She sobbed out a "thank you" and then continued to cry. I felt the tears come to my own eyes, and I wondered what suffering it was that had brought her here. I felt as if I ought to say or ask something, but I couldn't think of a thing; so I merely stood there with my arm around her shoulders.

For about ten minutes she continued to cry, and then her crying subsided and finally stopped. She pulled a tissue from her coat pocket and blew her nose several times. Her light brown hair was long and stringy, and she smelled like coffee. I still had not seen her face.

Finally, she squeezed my hand, turned and left. "Thank you so much," she whispered. Then she walked on back up the center aisle, toward the front door. I never saw her face. When she was finally out of view, I left the church and drove home.

I wanted to know more about the girl and her problem, but I realized I would probably never see her again. I also realized that before my breakdown, I would not have been drawn to comfort that girl. I would not have understood suffering.

Something was breaking through to me here: my own suffering had linked me to a part of the human condition outside of my previous experience. The girl and I were united by our common need for God even though we never did see each other's face. We were "one in the Spirit" just as surely as Father Dale and I had been in an earlier connection.

Eleven

*A*fter two weeks at Head Start, I heard through the grapevine of a very interesting opportunity. A large Protestant church in our community was looking for a Youth Director. The church was willing to consider a lay person.

I went quickly for an interview. The church was a downtown church, a large stone building in the Gothic style. The offices were well-furnished and comfortable, with quality carpeting and furniture. The senior pastor was composed and articulate. He interviewed me and said I was what they were looking for. The only hitch was that the position was half time, at half-time pay. My yearly salary would be something less than six thousand dollars. That was barely more than one quarter of the salary I had earned as a faculty member in New York.

But this was a job in Christian education—youth work—in a church. It was just what I wanted. Furthermore, the church also desired a part-time secretary, and they wanted to know if my wife might be interested.

I felt as though I had received an answer to my prayers. I thanked God for this opportunity. I was flooded with hope—more hope than I had felt for many, many months. When I told Judy about this development, she was as excited as I was; we threw our arms around each other.

I went to Mr. White at Head Start and told him about the church position; I told him I would have to leave Head Start. I felt guilty about leaving him.

"I knew you wouldn't be here long," he said. "I knew you were over-qualified when we hired you." But he was smiling.

I told him I was sorry for not staying longer.

"You're pretty good at the things you do, aren't you?" he said.

"I am?"

"Sure. The morale of these drivers is twice as high as it was before you came. And you've accomplished it in only two weeks."

There it was again. I felt no pride in what I had done at Head Start. I saw only the things I might have done better. It was the same message I had received again and again in therapy: I couldn't succeed. I was never good enough. I was simply not convinced of my own worth.

In October, Judy and I both began work at the church. I had much to learn, but I had my chance to serve God. I helped the young people of the church design and carry out their activities. We had educational experiences, recreational experiences, and service projects. We had canoe trips, pizza parties, guest speakers, worship services, and theatrical productions. We did work projects for the elderly members of the congregation.

Frequently we helped at the Champaign County Nursing Home. When we went to the home, we went with the staff to the individual rooms of the patients and brought them out to the recreation room. There we led the patients in activities that ranged from bingo to worship services. Being with the old and the lonely was a meaningful experience for our young people. They experienced misery and loneliness first hand, and they saw how hope and joy could be generated. I myself felt a special closeness to the elderly in the nursing home.

I spent a good deal of time calling the young people on the phone and visiting with them in their homes, getting to know them and their families. I discovered that my easy social skills made this part of my job comfortable.

In the church school program, I also had a role. I taught some classes and worked on teacher recruitment and training. I designed and led workshops for church school teachers. I was a good teacher with strong experience; I felt my contribution to the church school program was substantial.

During this period, my relationship with Jesus Christ was growing steadily. I went to our church sanctuary at some point in each working day and spent at least half an hour there, in prayer. Sometimes I read hymns silently to myself, sometimes out loud. I had favorite hymns, which I read prayerfully:

> I am Thine, O Lord, I have heard Thy voice,
> And it told Thy love to me;
> But I long to rise in the arms of faith,
> And be closer drawn to Thee.
> Draw me nearer, nearer blessed Lord,
> To the cross where Thou has died;
> Draw me nearer, nearer, nearer blessed Lord,
> To Thy precious, bleeding side.

"Take Time to be Holy" was another hymn that spoke directly to me:

> Take time to be holy,
> Let Him be thy Guide,
> And run not before Him,

Whatever betide;
In joy or in sorrow,
Still follow the Lord,
And, looking to Jesus,
Still trust in his Word.

I understood that the closest walk possible with Jesus Christ was not only the best path out of despair but the best path to fullness of life.

At other times I read from the book of worship or the Bible. Then I usually prayed silently, trying to rid my mind of intruding thoughts so that I could truly listen to the Lord.

My prayers in the sanctuary were like visits with a trusted and always reliable friend. Imagine—God was becoming my good friend. He listened to me, supported me, and cared for me. He did not cure my sufferings, nor did He take away my problems. At times I wished desperately that He would, and at those times I was impatient with Him. But I was beginning to understand that while I could trust God to be with me always, the resolution of my problems was up to me.

I had free will and choices. It would have been a great relief if the Lord had suddenly lifted my emotional problems from me, but I understood that His will could well be that it would remain up to me to lift them myself. I did not feel abandoned or let down by God; rather, I felt that He truly respected my courage, my willingness to work on solutions to my problems, and my commitment to a life of faith in Jesus Christ, His Son, *no matter what.*

I did not feel ashamed, or as if my faith were insufficient. I felt that God's continuing support would lead me to deeper faith, which was surely the final, best answer to ridding myself of emotional disorder. In short, although God did not eliminate my suffering, His continuous presence made me more and more aware of what I could do with His help.

I still had the anxiety problem, to be sure. I had chronic uneasiness and occasional sharp attacks of free-floating fears, even after two and a half years. Consequently, I worried. I worried about money and job security. I worried about my own emotional strength and my ability to keep going. I worried about many things.

I still tried to program every day, right to the hour. I guess it felt like control—anxiety attacks were certainly a lack of control. Free, unstructured time was still the enemy. I was not capable of spontaneity. My defense system had no provision for it. I was an authentic, generalized anxiety neurotic. I was still in jail. And, in fact, afraid to leave the cell.

The University of Illinois community had a wealth of activities that were the "absorbing" kind, the kind I could lose myself in. The athletic facilities were superb. I went running on the armory track nearly every day. I spent a good deal of time in Huff Gymnasium, playing basketball and working out in the weight room. I went to football games, basketball games, and gymnastic meets.

Jason and I went to hockey practice and hockey games together. We were thrilled by the color and fast action on the rink. And we often went to watch the University of Illinois marching band at practice. It was exciting, particularly to Jason, but also very special to me. Ever since my breakdown, when my very real fear was separation from him and Judy, I have cherished the opportunity to be with him and share activities with him.

Our work at the church was basically satisfying. Judy and I stayed there two years. During that time, there were a couple of serious problems we had to contend with.

The first was money. We were scraping by at the poverty level. Because my job was part-time, I always had to have a second source of income. Some semesters, I taught a course at Parkland College. That was a good second income and a stimulating opportunity. Some of the time, though, I was unable to get a course to teach. I worked other times at a swimming pool, doing painting and other maintenance work, such as cleaning and mowing. In the summers I went into the lawn-mowing business. I hauled my lawn mower around town and mowed lawns.

One afternoon, as I finished mowing one of my lawns, I sat down on the curb and looked at my situation. Here I was, thirty-four years old, with a master's degree and ten years of teaching experience at the college level. Two years earlier, I had been earning twenty thousand dollars a year. Now I was mowing lawns, as I had done twenty years earlier—my first job as a teen-ager! I wasn't particularly upset about this situation, although it did seem more than a little ironic, and I felt sorry for myself.

Our income was so low we were barely surviving from paycheck to paycheck. We were often in need of clothes and shoes. We walked as much as possible so as not to burn gasoline. We were robbing from the utility money to pay the rent, and vice-versa. The closest thing we experienced to a luxury was an occasional trip to the Dairy Queen. I'm sure we could have qualified for food stamps as well as other kinds of public assistance, but those kinds of opportunities never occurred to me. We did manage to keep Jason in his nursery school. Somehow, we always managed to pay for that.

This economic predicament began to take its toll on us. It did not frighten me, but it was very discouraging and frustrating. Judy was suffering. I came home one day and found her in tears.

My heart sank, and I put my arm around her. "I don't have enough money to buy the groceries we need," she sobbed.

"I know, I know," I said. "I can't get the car fixed either."

"I hate being this poor, but I don't want to whine about it. I know it won't be forever."

"I know it's bad," I said. I felt a powerful guilt.

She began to cry harder: "I need a coat and shoes; Jason needs a coat; he's only got that little baby thing, which doesn't fit, and anyway, it's much too cold for him to wear it!"

I felt a sadness inside on top of the guilt. My emotional disorder had caused us to rearrange our lives and had forced us to live in poverty. Or rather, I had *let* my disorder cause those changes. I didn't know what to say. After a while, her sobbing died down.

"I know it's not your fault," she said. "You didn't *make* yourself have a breakdown."

"But you can't help resenting me, can you?" I asked.

She started crying again, "I don't want to have any resentment, but I'm afraid I do."

"I don't blame you."

"I'm so ashamed to have any resentment," she said. "I know this is not your fault."

I put my arm around her again. I felt hollow inside, like a failure, a failure as a man, a husband, a person, and a father. My own life had spun out of control, and a consequence was this poverty and dislocation for my wife and son.

"I know this must make you feel terrible," she said.

"Yes, but maybe you need to say it," I said. "Maybe it's important for you to acknowledge it."

"Maybe, but I know it makes you feel terrible and I don't want you to. I want you to be proud of yourself for your courage and your determination."

I had a lump in my throat. I didn't say anything.

"I want you to feel proud of yourself, not guilty."

I brushed her hair back. She had stuck by me throughout the whole ordeal of these months and now years. "You have to resent this," I finally said. "You're a human being and you have to resent living like this. I resent my emotional disorder every day. You can't help having resentment, and there's nothing wrong with saying that you do."

"I don't want to make it harder for you," she said.

"You're not making it harder for me. I know it's there, and I need to hear it. It's good for me to recognize it. And for you." I understood her resentment and was suddenly feeling a certain relief from talking about it.

This was a difficulty Judy and I had to work on. She could not help resenting me even though she believed I was not at fault. Getting it out into the open was helpful. We talked about it frequently after that, trying always to identify and acknowledge our feelings, but trying to do so without placing any blame. My disorder had caused Judy to reorder her entire life; it was up to me to be continually aware of this and try to meet her emotional needs just as she had done for me for so long. The guilt I felt was not pleasant, but I knew I must not hide from the truth.

In addition to poverty, we found that our church was a second problem. Our church work tended to satisfy us in most respects, but it was not a church we would have attended had we not been employed there.

It was a large, "mainstream" church. The congregation was made up primarily of people in late middle age or older. We found the climate of the church to be cold and aloof. Most of the people merely came to church on Sunday morning and then went home. People did not relate to each other deeply or with intimacy. Most of the people in the congregation were formal and reserved. They were not comfortable with intimacy and seemed not to have an interest in developing any. Deeper relationships, or more honest ones, might have threatened them sharply. Yet, as far as I was concerned, breaking down barriers was a necessary part of the process of the Christian community as we had known it in upstate New York.

The church was not without its merit. It was financially sound, and the senior pastor's sermons were very instructive. We tried not to be negative, but we missed the intimate fellowship.

Judy and I talked often about those disappointments.

We tried to encourage a closer fellowship in church groups when possible, but the church was large and traditional, and very fixed in temperament. We also often admitted to ourselves that perhaps the church was what the congregation *wanted* it to be, although I knew well by this time how much people hurt and need to share the hurt.

We often talked of changing jobs again and getting into a different church, one more suited to our own needs. We really wanted some permanence and security, however; our lives had been disrupted and changed enough. We elected to stay with the church.

Twelve

Quite unexpectedly, in late summer of 1977, a new opportunity presented itself. Our conference, the Central Illinois Conference of the United Methodist Church, purchased East Bay Camp, a large youth camp and conference center. The camp was located on Lake Bloomington, near the twin cities of Bloomington-Normal, Illinois. Having been owned previously by several agencies jointly, it had recently gone into bankruptcy. As a high-school boy, I had held summer jobs at the camp, washing dishes, cleaning, mowing grass, and the like. I knew the camp well and had fond memories of it.

Our conference was now faced with the task of putting it on its feet again. Judy and I had done some camp counseling the previous summer, and we had met Rev. Steve Clapp, who was Conference Coordinator of Camping. Steve asked me if I would like to be part of the effort to re-establish the camp. The job he had in mind was to coordinate reservations and programming for the camp.

It would be a job with several responsibilities. The first would be to coordinate bookings for all groups who wanted to use the camp. The second would be to act as corresponding secretary. A third would be to act as contact person—to greet groups upon their arrival at camp, understand their needs, and try to help them meet those needs. A fourth would be to stimulate programming offered by the conference at the campsite and to design new, additional programming.

I discussed the opportunity with Judy; we were both very enthused. I quickly accepted the job. This meant another move, which we did not relish, but we packed up in another U-Haul truck and moved our belongings to a small house that stood on the grounds of the camp.

We were very happy with the location of our new home. We now lived on five hundred acres of woods and timber, bluffs and valleys. The bay was approximately one hundred yards to the south of our house. Everywhere around us there was nature to explore and trails to hike. Judy and I were both thrilled to realize that Jason would have the opportunity to grow up in such a setting. Within a week, we had hiked several times through the woods, identifying the shingle oaks, the sassafrass trees, the gingkoes, and the hawthornes.

Getting the camp back on its feet was not an especially difficult job. It had a rich history of service to church groups, school groups, and others throughout the state. Those of us at camp worked hard and were able to resurrect this history and make it a new reality.

The camp staff was a dedicated group. Everyone was willing to do what needed doing, even if it meant cleaning toilets or scrubbing floors. In fact, we were all grateful that we did not have the "luxury" of conventional job descriptions. All of my job-hunting made it plain to me how many people are trapped within the walls of restrictive job descriptions.

After some time at East Bay, I became the camp manager, which is the position I currently hold. It is a unique kind of work. At times the uniqueness is a blessing, at other times it is wearisome. There is no such thing as "quitting time" or "starting time." My life and my work are interwoven. In the spring, summer, and fall, I often work seven days a week, each day running from ten to sixteen hours. There are other employees who carry a similar workload. We plan our time as best we can, but the unexpected is always with us.

We might spend a day or two unplugging a troublesome sewer, felling a dead tree and cutting it for firewood, repairing broken windows, doors, toilets, or beds. There is always mowing, trimming, painting, landscaping, stump removal, bridge repair, dock repair, and boat repair. The lights burn out, the septic tanks have to be pumped, toilets, sinks, and floors have to be scrubbed, and roofs have to be repaired. During the night, we are often called out of bed to unplug a toilet, replace a blown fuse, deliver a coffeepot, or light a water heater. At moments like those, it is often difficult to keep in mind that this is service to the Lord, but I find it helpful if I can.

Yet, despite the workload, I cherish the job I have. I not only feel a part of the Christian community, but I also have a job that meets my emotional needs. It has always been important to me to be able to dictate, to some extent, the work that I do and the order in which I do it. Here at camp, I have that freedom more often than not. It has always been important for me to have some physical dimension to my work, to help me throw off emotional tension and anxiety. Here, I have that opportunity; there are always cleaning jobs, mowing jobs, and the like that need doing.

Also very gratifying is the sense of partnership that Judy and I have discovered here in this setting. Judy has pitched in and helped with the humdrum work; she has scrubbed pots and pans and stripped floors. She has also discovered some more creative outlets—she has managed the camp gift shop, helped with arts and crafts activities, and counseled young people in several different camping groups. She frequently answers the phone, takes messages, and plays a public relations role for the camp. Since our home is on camp grounds, we frequently resent the invasion of our privacy, which is an ongoing phenomenon; still, we do feel a sense of partnership. The work is something that involves both of us, together.

All three of us—Judy, Jason, and I—are active in the small United Methodist Church of Hudson, Illinois. Judy and I both teach Sunday school, and Judy has worked closely with children's choirs and dramatic productions in the church. Our church home is a good one.

We have done a good job for the camp. We have made a significant contribution here, a contribution beyond what many people could have done. I try to remind myself of this simple fact whenever I overlook something or make a mistake. I am learning to appreciate myself—I am lovable and capable—and so are you.

At East Bay Camp, we serve all kinds of church groups throughout the year. We serve Methodists, Presbyterians, Lutherans, Roman Catholics, Baptists, and many others. We also serve some school groups and community groups. We have the opportunity to work closely alongside countless directors and counselors.

We see groups coming together in community—getting away from the rat race of daily life and taking time to listen. We see groups coming together without television, radio, stereo, or telephone. Their resource is Jesus Christ; their opportunity is each other. We see people listening, caring, and loving. It is a *people* environment. People are more important than things.

Under those conditions, for a week or two, the deepest, most real kinds of relationships happen. Communities are born and grow to maturity. People are able to discover the rich love that can grow when they have time for God and for each other.

Those of us who work for the camping program are helping to make those things happen. As an employee of the camp, I feel I have a part in helping to build the Christian community. Most important, in this respect, I feel I have more than a job; I have a Christian vocation. With God's help, I have achieved an important goal.

In the five years that have passed since we became a part of East Bay Camp, my emotional problems have not disappeared. I am not a "together" or "cool" person. I may never become that type of person. I still have a low level of free-floating uneasiness that is more or less constant, even after these eight years.

Occasionally I have anxiety attacks that are relatively severe. When I do, I have confidence in my ability to deal with them. Occasionally I go for counseling help. We have a pastoral counseling center in Bloomington that operates in conjunction with Mennonite Hospital. The counselors are ordained Christian ministers with special training in psychology. They are supportive and encouraging of my Christian faith. When I do go for counseling, I don't go out of desperation. I no longer have an emotional disorder.

But I am still too tense. I still overreact to problems and blow them out of proportion. I still worry too much about things that are not worth worrying about. I am still too programmed, too dependent on structure. This remains the principal part of my emotional make-up that needs changing. I am now working to reduce my need for the rigid and busy system of defenses that I built to escape from terror. I need more spontaneity in my life—I need a stronger, healthier trust in myself to deal with life as it flows.

Reducing my need for rigid structure has proved to be a difficult task. I became so dependent on it, that I was a "structure addict": I could not live without it. I try each day to ease out of this dependence a little more.

But life is a process. I hope I can go on making progress. I have learned to like myself. I respect the person that I am, the person God created. I can do many things well, and I have much to give.

I've never really figured out, precisely, what happened to me those eight years ago. It's possible I never will. I don't know what, if anything in particular, triggered my breakdown. I don't know what overloaded my circuits.

I don't know if the things I did to fight back were the best. I do know that I fought a courageous fight, the best way I knew how. I'm not competely sure why I've gotten better. It's been a very slow process. If you paint the north wall and the south wall of a room enough times, eventually the two walls will meet. Sometimes I feel as if my progress is about that slow.

But it's still progress, even though I'm not altogether sure how I've made it. Maybe I've just outlasted the disorder through determination and will. Maybe I've retrained my central nervous system to withstand greater stress. No doubt the changes I've made in my life—particularly where honesty and truthfulness are concerned—have been important to my recovery.

I do know that, over the long haul, the stronger my relationship with Jesus Christ became, the stronger I felt as a person, and the less scary life became. My relationship with God, through Christ, progressed slowly. My first prayers were cries for help out of desperation; they did not include a relationship. The longer I continued my life of prayer, however, the more I felt in personal touch with God. The more real His presence became to me. The more I saw the love of Jesus Christ radiating from Dick Dutton and other devoted

Christians, the more I began to know the reality of a relationship with Christ for myself.

So even though I don't have all the answers nailed down, I do know this: I hope to walk this day with Jesus Christ, in His light, and take one more step out of the wilderness.

Epilogue

*T*hrough my breakdown and battle for recovery, I have learned a number of important lessons.

1. *I learned that Jesus Christ is a constant source of strength.* My growth as a Christian was one of the most important, permanent consequences of my struggle. My faith in God did not remove my suffering. There was no lightning bolt or parting of the waves. God did not reach down and remove my pain. He *did* come into my life and walk with me all the way on the long walk out of my desperate situation.

When we suffer, we want immediate relief. We want our problems to vanish immediately. We want books, pamphlets, formulas, and any other device that tells us there is a quick and easy solution to our problem. Discouraging as it may be, though, we need to remember that quick and easy is not always best. Some of the most enduring and substantial joys in life are the ones that come hard and take a long time to develop. When I turned to God, my suffering did not disappear—yet the slow path I walked with Him has had its own kind of beauty. It provided a sense of firmness and inevitable growth. It has unfolded and is still unfolding for me in a way that feels solid and enduring, like an ongoing miracle.

I do not believe that Satan was in me, causing all my troubles, although some have suggested that idea to me. I have no satisfactory answer to the problem of evil in the world, or why suffering exists; I am not a theologian. My personal belief is that suffering is inevitable in a world where people are fallen, are exercising free will, and are subject to natural law.

In the context of this belief, I do not believe that God either designed my suffering or caused it to be taken away. I believe my breakdown was a consequence of my living for thirty years without self-esteem; of twisting myself out of shape in an effort to win approval. My pattern in this respect probably overloaded my defense mechanisms to the point where they could no longer cope. In any case, I made my choices as I grew up among a number of other people who were also exercising their free will.

What I believe God does do for me, and will do for anyone, is to make His love available to me when I need it. I need it a lot, and I go to Him often. His love is manifest in the life of Jesus Christ. His love supports me and I know it is utterly reliable.

Many Christians suffer deeply for long periods of time. For reasons that God understands and we may not, He allows the suffering to continue. The protracted suffering does not mean that the sufferer has inadequate Christian faith. If our suffering does not disappear, it does not mean that our faith is weak. Even Jesus Himself suffered and was faced with difficult choices.

I know a young woman who has suffered with chronic mental disorder for a number of years; sometimes she is able to function successfully in the "real" world, at other times, not. Yet, she is a dedicated Christian. She is active in prayer groups and spends a good deal of her time in prayer for, and in service of, others. She is a giving and kind person, sincere, and active in church life. Everything I know about her tells me that she is an authentic Christian. Yet she continues to suffer and on two occasions has attempted suicide.

Last year a woman died in a nearby small town. I knew her well, and she was one of the most dedicated Christian persons I ever met. She died after suffering with cancer over a long period of time. Even as she was dying, she continued energetically in her church life and in her special kindnesses to people in need. I have no doubt that she prayed repeatedly for her suffering to be relieved. I have no doubt about the depth of her Christian faith. Still, she suffered and died.

An elderly man and woman are friends of mine on a nearby farm. They have been dedicated Christians for many years. They have continually suffered from assorted tragedies within their family. A few years ago, their youngest son, a man of twenty-eight with two small children, died of stomach cancer after several years of suffering and surgery. I well remember one Christmas Eve in church when this woman prayed at the altar, holding her small grandson to her tightly. I remember the tears running down my cheeks as I saw her there at the altar with such pain inside and her precious grandchild next to her. I have never known a more dedicated Christian than this woman, yet she suffered setbacks and tragedies.

We twist the meaning of Christian faith out of shape if we persist in thinking that those with strong love for the Lord Jesus Christ will know only bliss and happiness and material comfort. To be sure, the Holy Scriptures teach that the righteous will suffer—and know deliverance, too.

I do believe in miracles. At times, God seems to choose to climb right into our lives and activate a sudden reversal.

For reasons that He alone understands, the Lord may remove someone's suffering instantly.

I knew a young man some years ago who told me, "I got saved last night." It was evident to me that his life had indeed been suddenly reversed. Previously, he had been a drunk, shiftless, and frequently in jail. Now, he was alert, at peace, energetic, and purposeful. From that day on, his life changed. He became an active, serving Christian; today he is a full-time Christian pastor.

For others, however, even very dedicated Christians, a strong faith may not result in quick relief. This does not automatically mean that such people have inadequate faith. God works uniquely with each of us.

2. *I believe in the protection of the Christian community.* Christians need better communities. We are hurting people—lonely, afraid, and dislocated. Our culture is so fast-paced and impersonal that our traditional communities, schools, families, and even churches are disappearing. People in our culture feel lonely and alienated. We need a revival of Christian community.

I once read in the *New York Times* of a family in Dearborn, Michigan. Each morning, the father went to work in Detroit. The mother went to work in a neighboring suburb. The son was bused to school in another suburb, and the daughter stayed in Dearborn to go to school. Each of the four members of the family was involved in a different community each day. They did not see or know the same people. They did not share any friends, colleagues, or schoolmates. They did not experience community. None at all. How could they feel a part of anything, much less the *same* thing?

Millions of people throughout our culture experience the same kind of dislocation every day. Their anxieties are evident in millions of tranquilizers, wealthy analysts, liquor consumption, aggression, lawsuits, depression, and violence. In our culture, we are desperate for the support system of *real* communities—groupings where we feel accepted, loved, and cared for; where we build trust and love by taking time for one another.

We experienced a taste of that kind of community in our house church in New York. God's love was the spine of our church. Within Christ's love, we were able to love and care for one another patiently. We had time for one another. We had an alternative to the fragmentation of our culture.

At East Bay Camp we see many groups—children, youth, and adults—coming together in a loving Christian fellowship. They may only be together for a weekend, or a week, or two weeks. But at least for that period of time, they can experience the deepest kind of closeness. It can happen. It is possible.

Many people do not find such an alternative in their church life. They often find loneliness and impersonality even in their church. The church mirrors the rest of the culture. I personally think it is vital for Christian people to begin to view their church community as a potentially superior kind of community, and work toward that end. Pastors and church leaders must see their roles as fathers and mothers in a family, and bring intimacy and care back into the church.

3. *Psychotherapy has limitations, yet it is worthwhile and we should make use of it.* There is much that analysts and therapists do not understand about people and why they do the things they do. Most therapists and analysts admit this readily. There is wide disagreement among those who practice therapy as to what is effective therapy and what is not. There are Freudians, Behaviorists, and Humanists, and others. There are those who regard religion as crucial, and those who regard it as an unhealthy crutch. Therapists do not agree.

This means that when we hurt, psychotherapy may or

may not provide us with the best answers. The psychotherapist may be just as baffled as we are. Yet I believe that psychotherapy is something we should use. My own experience with Dick Dutton, Father Dale, and others, tells me that therapy *in connection with* the community of faith is the best answer for emotional disorder. This combination of elements—creative listening and Christian care—was vital to the progress I made.

A good therapist is a good listener, and I needed to be in touch with good listeners. Whether we suffer deeply or not, most of us are hungry for listeners. There's something relieving and affirming about being listened to. It tends to affirm our worth as persons; at least it always did for me. Pastors and other Christians can be good listeners, and it's important for them to make a priority of this if they want their church to be a real Christian community.

Psychotherapy helped me identify and speak the truth. Before my breakdown, a great deal of my life had been a lie. Learning something of therapeutic method—asking tough questions simply—helped me pierce the smokescreen and camouflage of my own life. I learned to identify my own feelings in simple terms and to speak them simply. "I feel afraid." "I feel lonely." "When this happens I feel guilty." And so on.

This seems simple enough, yet for me it was not. I had been living for too long on a level of distortion and artifice that confused me. Psychotherapy helped me identify my real feelings.

Psychotherapy helped me to know myself. As I began to recognize the truth about myself and acknowledge it, I began to understand who I was (am). Psychotherapy did not provide me with any quick answers or any easy way out of my suffering, but step by step I began to understand myself. As I began to learn who I was, I began to have a basis for appreciating myself.

4. *With the Lord's help, I can survive.* I suffered foɪ

months and months under acute, mystifying stress. Still, I found my survival skills were strong enough to carry me to the other side. Many times, I wanted to quit. I wanted to give up. But I never did—I never missed a single class, meeting, or responsibility.

If you are suffering, maybe your survival skills are stronger than you think. If you suffer from grief, anxiety, depression, apprehension, or disorientation, you may doubt your ability to go on coping. Perhaps you are stronger than you think.

If you are a Christian, let God help you. Even if the problems don't disappear, keep trusting Jesus Christ with your whole life. If you walk this difficult road knowing that He is with you, the trip will be easier.

My understanding of the love of God was the underpinning that kept me fighting the good fight. Once I experienced this love through Christ, I was no longer merely surviving *from* something, I was surviving *into* something. I was more and more aware of my own worth. Our suffering, no matter how disabling, does not negate our goodness as people or our worth as people. God loves us deeply, *wherever we are.* I was able to keep this in mind, somehow, and it fortified me all the way.

I have an early morning routine that I often practice here at camp, particularly during the summer, when life is so hectic. Just at sunrise I take my Bible and go sit beneath a huge white oak tree just south of our house. From there, I can see our bay and the old wooden footbridge that spans it.

It is very quiet. Even the dining hall staff are not yet at work. I can hear the occasional voice of an early-rising camper from across the bay. Otherwise, the only sounds are those that the birds make.

In this peaceful environment, I often read portions of

the life of Jesus or a few of the Psalms. I revel for a time in the quiet, reassuring presence of the Lord, for in a short time there will be an abundance of noise and activity.

I open my Bible and read, "The LORD is my shepherd." And I believe it.